queso!

queso!

Regional recipes for
the world's favorite
chile-cheese dip

LISA FAIN

photography by Aubrie Pick

TEN SPEED PRESS
California | New York

Copyright © 2017 by Lisa Fain
Photographs copyright © 2017 by Aubrie Pick

Published in the United States by Ten Speed Press,
an imprint of the Crown Publishing Group, a division
of Penguin Random House LLC, New York.
www.crownpublishing.com
www.tenspeed.com

Ten Speed Press and the Ten Speed Press
colophon are registered trademarks of Penguin
Random House LLC.

Library of Congress Cataloging-in-Publication
Data is on file with the publisher.

Hardcover ISBN: 978-0-399-57951-6
eBook ISBN: 978-0-39957-952-3

Printed in China

Design by Margaux Keres
Food styling by Lillian Kang
Props by Claire Mack

10 9 8 7 6 5 4 3 2

First Edition

For my dear Texan friends who have
shared numerous bowls of queso with
me over the years. Here's to making
more mighty fine memories together.

CONTENTS

INTRODUCTION

For the lover of chile con queso, or simply "queso" as the dish is more affectionately known, it's not unusual to find yourself eating it several times in a single day. Take, for example, my experience on a trip to Austin a few years ago. After scooping tortilla chips into bowls of this molten mix of chiles and cheese at both breakfast and lunch, that evening I found myself at a friend's house enjoying, yes, even more queso. (She had also made Frito pies, so there was some variety in my diet.) Eating the same thing three times in one day may seem excessive to some, but it was not a problem for me. In my experience, there is no such thing as too much queso.

My friend had made the standard party recipe—a can of tomatoes with green chiles heated with a one-pound brick of processed cheese food until melted. Most of you know what I'm talking about and agree that this is fine stuff. Food snobs may turn up their noses, but that's their loss.

As the night progressed, I observed that we were all gathered around the slow cooker. And as we took turns dipping our chips into the golden elixir, there was much connecting, sharing, and laughter. Life wasn't perfect but our fellowship helped us to pause for a moment and put the bad away. That night, like many nights, queso not only brought us together but it also brought joy into our lives.

For the uninitiated, chile con queso is an addictive blend of chiles and melted cheese that is ubiquitous in the Southwest. Although it's typically served as a creamy dip, there are variations in which it's spooned into soft tortillas or even eaten with a fork. No matter its form, however, it is always happy food for all seasons and occasions, and it's the odd get-together

that doesn't have it on hand for people to share. Queso is always a welcome guest.

Now, as a Texan I grew up eating chile con queso, but I will confess that I didn't think too much about it until I moved to New York for work when I was twenty-five. It was there I learned that outside the Southwest, it is difficult to find the building blocks to classic queso, so I would have to improvise with what was available. As I researched recipes, I discovered there was a whole world beyond canned tomatoes and brick cheese. For instance, a friend from El Paso told me that the chile con queso along the border was very different from the American-cheese versions found in the rest of the state and beyond. Curious, on my next trip home I visited this city in the far western corner of the state and learned that indeed, there and in nearby southern New Mexico, queso is made with long green chiles and white melting cheeses, much like how it's served across the border in the Mexican state of Chihuahua. This was a revelation.

After that initial visit to El Paso, I became obsessed with learning more about the history and regional variations of chile con queso, but discovered not much had been written on the topic, not even a book. So that night at my friend's house in Austin, when I was asked what I planned to write about next, inspired by the queso and the camaraderie, I told my friends I wanted to explore chile con queso in more depth. They agreed it was a fine idea and a few months later, I hit the road to learn more.

I returned to El Paso and then drove along the Texas-Mexico border, following the Rio Grande toward the Gulf of Mexico, eating chile con queso along the way. I noticed how the quesos would vary from town to town, each different from the next. For instance, in the north, the quesos were creamier and well suited for chips, but farther south, closer to the Gulf of Mexico, substantial skillet quesos known as queso fundido or queso flameado were the prevailing style, dishes so thick that tortillas were needed instead.

Despite the variations in chile con queso along the border, they still felt connected to the dish's Mexican roots. It wasn't until I arrived in the South Texas coastal city of Corpus Christi that I began to see the Tex-Mex rendition made with processed American cheese. Although this Tex-Mex bowl of gold, as it's often called, is widespread throughout the rest of the state and beyond, there is still much room for innovation. So in larger cities such as Austin and Houston, there are quirky versions that embrace the state's changing demographics and culinary landscape, such as queso made with Indian chutney and plant-based quesos, too.

Curious about the dish's history, I spent time at the library reading periodicals and cookbooks in an attempt to piece together chile con queso's origins and evolution. And then there were the moments when queso appeared in unexpected places, such as at an ice cream stand in New Mexico and on a plate of chicken-fried steak in San Antonio.

This book explores queso's many historical and geographical varieties. An Austinite might not recognize what is being served as chile con queso in El Paso because the local queso styles are vastly different. But they do share a lineage and a name, so though they may be distant cousins, they are still family at heart.

As I drove across the Southwest discovering, researching, talking, and eating all things queso, everyone I met would light up and share a story with me. With queso, it is easy to make new friends. My guess is you're holding this book because you, too, love queso and want to learn more. You've come to the right place. I've collected an array of recipes that celebrate queso in all its velvety, spicy, and special glory. So gather your loved ones and pull out the chiles and cheese. I know you'll have a good time because queso is a joyful food that makes everyone happy. This is the power of queso.

Vehicles

Tortilla chips are the preferred dippers for most quesos, as are tortillas, both flour and corn. Historical recipes often called for toast or saltine crackers—a bit odd by today's standards but still delicious. And if you're feeling healthy, vegetables are an option, too.

THE CHILE CON QUESO KITCHEN

If you're like me, you probably want to enjoy chile con queso all the time. These are the key items I keep on hand so I can make a batch whenever the urge strikes.

CHILES

Chiles are equal partners in chile con queso, and without them you would just have cheese. There is a vast world of chiles, but these are the ones most commonly used in queso.

Fresh Chiles

Fresh chiles are the most common chiles used for making queso, as their bright, vegetal tones are a good foil for the rich and creamy cheese. In the past, they were available only during their growing season, which is late summer through early fall. These days, however, you can find them year-round. When buying fresh chiles, look for ones that are fragrant with firm, bright skin. Avoid those with soft spots, but if the chiles have white lines running through the skin that is fine as it just shows that the chile has been on the plant for a long time and will likely be hotter. To store them, keep fresh chiles in the refrigerator for 1 week. The chile's heat comes from the seeds and the veins, which I remove. If you want a spicier experience, then don't remove them.

ANAHEIM, HATCH, AND NEW MEXICO CHILES are long, green chiles with a pointed tip and heat that can range from mild to hot. Their skin is thick, so these chiles needs to be roasted and peeled before eating. If you can't find these types or want to save time, 4 ounces of canned green chiles equals 2 roasted and peeled fresh chiles, but also know that chiles you roast yourself are much more flavorful.

HABANEROS are small, lantern-shaped chiles that are extremely fiery. They usually come in festive colors such as red, yellow, and orange, and have a fruity, bright flavor.

JALAPEÑOS are the unofficial chile of the state of Texas. Short, thick, and green with a pointed tip, the chiles have a fresh, vegetal flavor with a spicy bite, though sometimes you find mild ones, too.

POBLANOS are dark green, dagger-shaped chiles with a robust green flavor that can range from mild to medium hot. They are usually roasted and peeled before using.

SERRANOS are narrow, short, pointed green chiles that have a fierce bite. They are not as hot as habaneros, but are more fiery than jalapeños.

Roasting Fresh Chiles

Because of their thick skin, some fresh chiles need to be roasted and peeled before using. Here is how to do that: In a large, ovenproof skillet or on a baking sheet, place the chiles under the broiler 6 inches from the heating element. Cook until blackened, about 5 minutes per side. Place the chiles in a paper sack or plastic food-storage bag, close it tightly, and let it steam for 20 minutes. To peel the chiles, remove them from the bag and gently rub off the skin.

Dried Whole Chiles

As the name implies, these are chiles that have been dried whole. Their flavors are more earthy and intense than their fresh counterparts. When buying whole dried chiles, look for ones that are tender and pliable like a raisin. You should store each type of chile separate from one another in an airtight container to keep the flavors pure. They can last for up to 1 year.

ANCHO CHILES are the dried poblano chiles, and they have an earthy, bittersweet flavor.

CHIPOTLE CHILES are smoked jalapeños. They are most commonly sold in cans, packed in a flavorful sauce called adobo that is made with tomatoes and vinegar. If you are using chipotle chiles in adobo, you do not need to rehydrate them.

PEQUÍN CHILES are tiny, oval chiles that grow wild in northern Mexico, Texas, and New Mexico. They are fiery and a little goes a long way. The fresh ones are hard to find outside the Southwest, but dried ones are more widely available. If you can't find them, a small pinch of cayenne will suffice for each pequín chile that the recipe calls for.

Rehydrating Dried Chiles

Dried chiles need to be rehydrated before use. To do this, remove and discard the stems and seeds and cook the chiles in a dry cast-iron skillet over medium heat for 5 to 10 seconds, flipping them once. Pour in water to cover, bring to a simmer, then turn off the heat. Let soak for 30 minutes, until the chiles are soft and plump. To use, remove the chiles from the water and rinse well (the soaking water can be bitter).

Ground Chiles

Dried chiles that have been ground into a powder make it easy to add a quick hit of flavor to your dish.

CAYENNE is a familiar hot spice that adds a fresh, bright heat and helps amplify other flavors as well.

CHILI POWDER is a combination of ancho chiles, oregano, garlic, allspice, and clove. This particular flavor profile is the essence of Tex-Mex food and cooking.

PAPRIKA, an earthy, red chile powder, is usually mild but can sometimes be hot.

SMOKED PAPRIKA, a Spanish specialty, is made from chiles that are dried over smoke, which gives them a fire-kissed flavor. Smoked paprika is sometimes called by its Spanish name, *pimentón*, and is sold in sweet, bittersweet, and hot varieties, although sweet is the most common.

CHEESE

The other partner in chile con queso is the cheese. From Mexican white melting cheeses to American processed cheese, here are the cheeses used in this book. **It's very important that you buy chunks or blocks and grate the cheese yourself**, as pre-packaged shredded cheese is mixed with non-clumping agents that prevent the cheese from melting into a smooth sauce.

ASADERO This is a semihard, slightly tangy white cheese found in northern Mexico that melts easily. Substitutions are Chihuahua, Muenster, and Monterey Jack.

CHEDDAR This semisoft cheese can come in many different guises. When young, it's softer and milder, when aged it becomes crumbly and nuttier. Typically, Texan cuisine calls for younger Cheddar cheese that is orange in color as it's been dyed by annatto seeds. Cheddar melts very well.

CHIHUAHUA A semihard, creamy white cheese that hails from the Mexican state with the same name. It's also known as queso Menonita, as it was originally made by Mennonite settlers in Chihuahua.

COTIJA This crumbly, grainy Mexican cheese has a salty, slightly nutty flavor. It's usually sold in blocks and to use, you just pinch off what you need and then crumble it into the dish, mostly as a garnish. If you can't find cotija, feta makes a good substitute.

FETA A salty, tangy brined cheese that crumbles easily. In Greece, the cheese has to be made with sheep's milk or a combination of sheep's and goat's milk in order to be classified as feta, though outside the country there are cow's milk versions, too.

GOUDA A Dutch cheese that can come in many varieties, from semihard to hard. For queso, a semihard version is best. It's sweet, creamy, and melts well.

GRUYÈRE A hard Swiss cheese that is nutty and salty. Before people in Mexico developed and produced their own cheeses, this was popular and widely used.

MONTEREY JACK This soft, creamy cheese has a simple, milky flavor. It melts very well. It was developed by Spanish friars at their California missions near Monterey in the mid-1800s, then later marketed by a man named David Jacks in the 1890s. **Colby Jack** is a blended cheese that is a mild Cheddar and Jack combination.

MUENSTER This white, semisoft cheese has a mild, slightly tangy flavor that is very similar to young Mexican cheeses such as asadero. It melts smoothly.

PANELA A semifirm, fresh-milk cheese with a creamy, mild flavor. It's excellent for frying as it holds its shape when heat is applied and develops a crisp shell. Good substitutions are haloumi and paneer.

PROCESSED CHEESE There are two types of processed cheese used in the book—American cheese and brick processed cheese. Here's the difference:

American cheese is a blend of cheeses such as Cheddar and Monterey Jack mixed with oils, milk, and emulsifiers. It's a semifirm cheese that has a low melting point, which makes it ideal for Tex-Mex chile con queso, though it does need liquid and/or starch to hold it together in a smooth sauce. Because it's usually sold pre-packaged in individual slices, it's easier and more economical, when making queso, to buy it by the pound at your store's deli counter.

Brick processed cheese, on the other hand, is the product most know as Velveeta, though there are other brands. It is a mixture of various cheeses, oils, and stabilizers that doesn't have enough dairy to legally be called cheese, so instead it's classified as "cheese food." No matter, because of these qualities, it's amazing for queso as it doesn't need any extra stabilizers to melt smoothly.

QUESO FRESCO A Mexican fresh cheese that is mild and crumbles easily. Depending on how it's made, when heat is applied some brands may melt completely and become creamy but others will retain small curds.

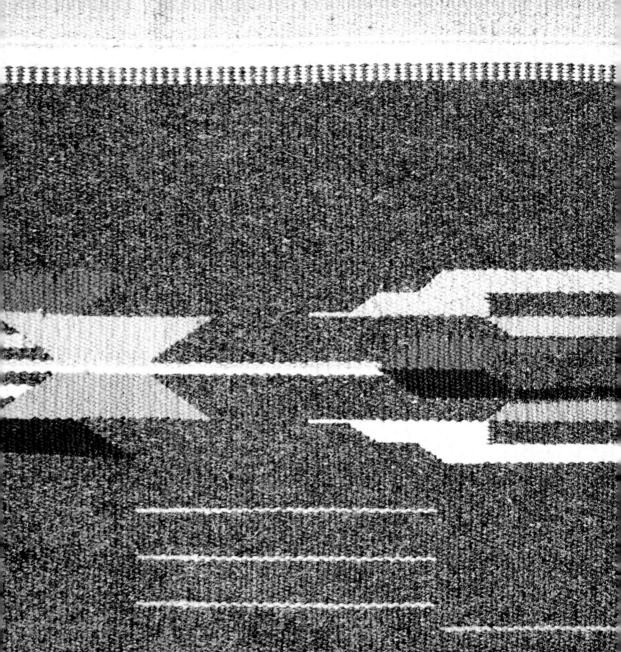

CHILE CON QUESO, THE EARLY YEARS

In the late 1500s, Spanish explorers arrived in the area around what is known today as El Paso, Texas, along the Mexican-American border. With them, they brought livestock, such as cows and goats, which that part of the world had never seen. Dairy was not known to the Native Americans, as their diet was made up of indigenous ingredients such as corn, squash, and chiles. From that point, however, as the old world connected with the new, it was perhaps inevitable that one day cheese would be paired with chiles and a culinary alliance would be born.

Although the exact moment when chile con queso came into existence has not been determined, the earliest reference to it in print can be found in the 1816 Mexican novel, *El Periquillo Sarniento* (*The Mangy Parrot*) by José Joaquín Fernández de Lizardi. The next citation occurred in 1865 in the Mexican poem "Glosa del Chile Verde con Queso," in which an anonymous poet laments that women of his era know much about artifice and fashion but little about practical matters such as stewing chiles with cheese.

Despite the presence of chile con queso in the literature of the day, Mexican cookbooks from the 1800s did not feature recipes with that name, though dishes composed of chiles with cheese did exist. One such recipe, Chiles Poblanos, found in the 1887 cookbook *La Cocinera Poblana*, was made up of poblano chiles, cheese, and tomatoes.

Although chile con queso most likely originated in Mexico, the first published recipe to use the phrase appeared in the United States. An 1896 article about

Mexican cuisine in the magazine *The Land of Sunshine* included a dish called Chiles Verdes con Queso, which was a mixture of long green chiles, tomatoes, and cheese. Like all early Mexican versions, it was intended to be a side dish, with the cheese enhancing the chiles, much like cheese melted onto cauliflower. Its evolution to a dip was yet to come.

Now, looking toward Europe, Swiss fondue and its British counterpart, Welsh rarebit (or rabbit), became popular in the United States in the late 1800s. Fondue is a pot of melted cheese for dipping bread and vegetables; Welsh rarebit is a melted cheese dish that is poured over toast. Neither was considered a side dish but instead was an appetizer or the main event of a meal.

Then, in 1908, a Kentucky newspaper ran a recipe for Mexican rarebit, a take on Welsh rarebit that added chile pulp to a base of melted cheese, milk, and egg and was served over toast. In 1909, the San Francisco newspaper *Call* published a similar recipe, but replaced the chile pulp with chili powder, a blend of ground ancho chiles with herbs and spices, such as oregano and cumin. One of the fathers of chili powder was a German immigrant in Texas named William Gebhardt. He began to market his Eagle Brand chili powder in 1896, and in 1911 his company produced a cookbook that included a recipe for Mexican rarebit similar to the San Francisco version.

About the same time, recipes for and references to Mexican chile con queso began appearing more frequently in the press. Eventually, an astute cook realized that combining rarebit (and getting rid of the egg often used in its preparation) and chile con queso would make for a fine dish, which leads us to a recipe for Mexican rarebit that appeared in the 1914 edition of *Boston Cooking School Magazine* and that called for green chiles, tomatoes, cheese, beer, and corn. This version, though intended for pouring over toast, was very close to what most would consider American chile con queso today.

In Texas, chile con queso appeared in restaurants as early as 1910, when San Antonio's Gunter Hotel offered it, according to the book *The Menu Maker*. (In 1922, O. M. Farnsworth asserted that the menu for his Original Mexican Restaurant, also in San Antonio, had not changed since it opened in 1900. Chile con queso was on the menu at the time, so perhaps it was served back in 1900, though no one seems to have documents to confirm this.) It is not known what form this dish took—whether it was a side dish or a sauce to be poured over tostadas or toast.

Then, in the early 1920s, a recipe with the name Chile con Queso appeared in the *Woman's Club Cook Book of Tested and Tried Recipes* published by the Woman's Club of San Antonio. Like some Mexican rarebit recipes, this chile con queso used cayenne and paprika instead of the fresh chiles found in Mexican chile con queso. But it did not contain egg and it was the first chile con queso recipe to call specifically for American cheese. A truly American queso in both name and style had arrived.

After that, chile con queso appeared frequently in Texas publications and community cookbooks. These early recipes were served over toast or tostadas or were enjoyed as dips with potato chips, crackers, tostadas, or Fritos, after their invention in 1932. American cheese was a popular choice in these early recipes; Velveeta, which was invented in 1918 but not widely marketed until later, didn't make its first appearance in a queso recipe until 1939, in *What'll I Cook?* published by the First Christian Church of Lubbock.

In 1943, Carl Roetelle opened his canning plant in Elsa, Texas, and began to market Ro-Tel tomatoes, which were tomatoes blended with green chiles. Then in 1949, a Ro-Tel ad appeared with a recipe for making a chile con queso by simply heating a can of the spicy tomatoes with American or processed cheese until melted, and serving the dip with toasted tortillas or Fritos: a Tex-Mex classic was born.

While most of Texas was enjoying chile con queso made with American cheese, green chiles, and tomatoes, in the area around El Paso and southern New Mexico, the dish with that name had more in common with what was found across the border in the Mexican state of Chihuahua. It wasn't meant to be just a side dish any longer, however, as it was also served as an appetizer with tortilla chips and tortillas, much like it was across the rest of Texas.

Chile con queso, in all its forms and permutations, was still very much a regional specialty when First Lady Claudia "Lady Bird" Johnson shared her version in the *Washington Post* in 1964. Despite the attention, the dish wasn't popularized, though people in the Southwest, Texas, and Midwest continued to make queso. In these regions, it became a staple at social gatherings. There wasn't much variation in the recipes, however, until recent years, when creative cooks took the basic formula and crafted it into something new.

The history of chile con queso is rich and varied, much like the dish itself. In this chapter, I've included recipes that show the beginnings and evolution of this uniquely North American blend of the Old World and New. Admittedly, a couple of the recipes are included for their historical significance and not their tastiness. I've shown how they were originally written, and also given suggestions on how to adapt them to today's tastes, so be sure to read the headnotes before making the recipes. That said, most of these recipes are as fresh and inviting to people today as they were over one hundred years ago.

1 tablespoon
unsalted butter

1½ cups diced
grape tomatoes

4 poblano chiles,
roasted (see page 3),
peeled, seeded, and
cut into thin slices

¼ cup whole milk

4 ounces Gruyère
or asadero cheese,
shredded

¼ teaspoon kosher salt

Warm corn or flour
tortillas, for serving

Researching queso for this book, I spent a day at the University of Texas at San Antonio reading Mexican cookbooks from the 1800s, and this was the earliest published recipe I could find that resembled chile con queso.

The original ingredients list called simply for "cheese" without being more specific, so I guessed at the intent. Asadero, a mild melting cheese, was available in the late 1800s and worked well when I tried it in the dish. I also made the recipe with Gruyère, another cheese popular in Mexico at the time, and found I preferred its nutty, salty flavor with the earthy peppers. Like many Mexican chile con quesos, this dish is meant to be served as a side dish but it's satisfying wrapped in tortillas, too.

CHILES POBLANO

1887 // MAKES 4 SERVINGS

In a large skillet, melt the butter over low heat. Add the tomatoes and cook, stirring occasionally, until softened and some of the juices have been released, about 5 minutes. Stir in the poblanos and cook for 1 to 2 minutes longer, or until fragrant and warm. Stir in the milk, cheese, and salt. Cook, stirring, until the cheese has melted, 1 to 2 minutes. Taste and add more salt, if you like.

Serve immediately as a side dish or with warm tortillas.

20 Anaheim chiles

4 ripe plum tomatoes, halved lengthwise

1 tablespoon lard, shortening, or vegetable oil

8 ounces Monterey Jack cheese, shredded

¼ teaspoon kosher salt

Warm corn or flour tortillas, for serving

The earliest published recipe for chile con queso appeared in 1896 in *The Land of Sunshine* (a magazine published in Los Angeles). Prior to this, the term had been used in Mexican literature and recipes had appeared that were similar to the dish, but this is the first recipe with the phrase "chile con queso" in the name.

The recipe, like many early ones, did not specify a type of cheese, so I assumed Monterey Jack because that cheese was created in California by Mexican Franciscan monks in the mid-1800s.

This queso's simplicity is part of its charm. It's too thick to be a dip, but makes for a hearty side dish folded into tortillas.

▼▲▼▲▼▲▼▲▼▲▼▲▼▲▼▲▼▲▼▲▼▲▼

CHILE VERDE CON QUESO

1896 // MAKES 4 TO 6 SERVINGS

Line a baking sheet with aluminum foil. Position a rack about 6 inches from the upper heating element and preheat the broiler. Place the Anaheims and tomatoes, skin-side up, on the sheet. Roast, turning once, for 10 minutes, or until the skins are blackened.

Transfer the chiles to a paper sack or plastic food-storage bag, close it tightly, and let the chiles steam for 20 minutes. Remove the chiles from the bag and rub off the skins. Discard the stems and seeds and dice the chiles. Rub off the skins from the tomatoes.

In a large skillet, melt the lard over medium-low heat and add the chiles and tomatoes. Gently mash with the back of a wooden spoon and cook until heated through and fragrant, about 5 minutes. Add the cheese and cook, stirring, until melted. Add the salt, then taste and add more salt, if you like.

Serve immediately as a side dish or with warm tortillas.

2 tablespoons unsalted butter

¾ cup diced grape tomatoes

2 Anaheim chiles, roasted (see page 3), peeled, seeded, and diced

¼ cup fresh or frozen corn kernels

½ cup Mexican lager, such as Modelo Light

8 ounces yellow American cheese, shredded

½ teaspoon cayenne

½ teaspoon kosher salt

Toast or Tortilla Chips (page 128), for serving

In 1914, *Boston Cooking School Magazine* published a recipe for Mexican rarebit that both eliminated the egg, typically part of the recipe, and included fresh green chiles, tomato, and corn. The recipe tastes surprisingly current today, and if I had to cite a recipe that marked the transition to what Americans now know as chile con queso, this would be the one. If you're feeling old-fashioned, serve it over toast as it was originally intended, but it's terrific with tortilla chips, too.

▽△▽△▽△▽△▽△▽△▽△▽△▽△▽△▽

MEXICAN RAREBIT

1914 // MAKES 4 TO 6 SERVINGS

In a medium saucepan, melt the butter over medium-low heat. Add the tomatoes, Anaheims, and corn and cook, stirring occasionally, until some of the juices have been released from the tomatoes, about 2 minutes.

Pour in the beer and add the cheese. Cook, stirring, until the cheese has melted and the sauce is creamy. (If it seems too thick, you can add more beer.) Stir in the cayenne and salt. Taste and adjust the seasonings, if you like.

Serve immediately over toast or with tortilla chips.

1 pound yellow American cheese, shredded

½ cup whole milk

2 teaspoons paprika

1 teaspoon cayenne

½ teaspoon kosher salt

Toast, for serving

The first recipe published in Texas with the name "chile con queso" appeared in the early 1920s in the *Woman's Club Cook Book of Tested and Tried Recipes* published by the San Antonio Woman's Club. The chiles in this version are not fresh and green but instead are spoonfuls of dried red cayenne and paprika. Another quirk is that instead of being served with tortilla chips, this recipe is poured over toast, a common way at the time to serve melted cheese dishes. I will admit I'm sharing this recipe more as a historical curiosity than as an exciting eating experience—it's not the most lively queso, but it does provide insight into how the beloved dish has evolved. If you took this recipe and threw in some green chiles and tomatoes, you'd be well on your way to what we recognize as Tex-Mex queso today.

SAN ANTONIO CHILE CON QUESO

EARLY 1920S // MAKES 6 TO 8 SERVINGS

In a medium saucepan, combine the cheese, milk, paprika, cayenne, and salt. Cook over low heat, stirring, until the until the cheese has melted and the queso is smooth. Taste and adjust the seasonings, if you like.

Serve immediately over toast.

1 tablespoon lard
or vegetable oil

12 Anaheim chiles,
roasted (see page 3),
peeled, seeded, and
finely chopped

2 cups finely chopped
cooked steak, pork,
or chicken

1½ cups diced grape
tomatoes

1½ cups beef broth
or chicken broth

4 ounces Monterey Jack
cheese, shredded

Kosher salt

Warm flour tortillas,
for serving

The *El Paso Herald* in 1923 described this early recipe as "a famous old Mexican recipe for chili con queso, a dish as popular with Americans in El Paso as with the Mexican folk." What's interesting about it is that it calls for meat, which was unusual for queso recipes at the time. At first I thought that the spelling of the dish—"chili con queso"—was simply a mistake, as *chili* refers to the meaty stew while *chile* refers to the pepper. But I made the recipe and discovered the dish is so hearty that the spelling may have been intentional. It's good scooped into warm tortillas and also substantial enough that one could eat it in a bowl with a spoon.

EL PASO CHILI CON QUESO

1923 // MAKES 6 TO 8 SERVINGS

In a large skillet, melt the lard over medium-low heat. Add the Anaheims, meat, and tomatoes and cook, stirring occasionally, until the tomatoes are just beginning to break down and release their juices, 3 to 5 minutes.

Pour in the broth, then add the cheese. Cook without stirring until the cheese has melted, a couple of minutes. Add salt to taste.

Serve immediately with warm tortillas.

4 tablespoons
unsalted butter

¼ cup all-purpose flour

2 cups whole milk

1 pound yellow American
cheese, shredded

1 teaspoon ketchup

1 teaspoon hot pepper
sauce, such as Tabasco

1 teaspoon chili powder

1 teaspoon paprika

1 teaspoon ground
cumin

1 teaspoon cayenne

1 teaspoon granulated
garlic

½ teaspoon powdered
mustard

¼ teaspoon cumin seeds

Kosher salt

Pickled Jalapeños
(page 126), for garnish

Tortilla Chips (page 128),
for serving

In 1938, W. F. "Blackie" and Margaret Donnelly opened Mexico Chiquito in Little Rock, Arkansas. These two Texans brought their restaurant concept across state lines from the town of Kilgore, where they opened the original Mexico Chiquito in 1936. It was perhaps the first restaurant to call the concoction we know as chile con queso "cheese dip," the term preferred by folks in Arkansas, and both the restaurant and its dip are still beloved in the state today.

This recipe is adapted from one attributed to the restaurant, but because its authenticity has been debated, I opted to call my version Arkansas Cheese Dip. With its inclusion of ketchup and powdered mustard, this dip hearkens back to other melted cheese dishes from the 1930s. Topped with pickled jalapeños, it takes on a tangy, slightly sweet flavor that makes it excellent on hot dogs and hamburgers.

▼△▼△▼△▼△▼△▼△▼△▼△▼△▼△▼△▼△▼△

ARKANSAS CHEESE DIP

1930s // MAKES 6 TO 8 SERVINGS

In a medium saucepan, melt the butter over low heat. Whisk in the flour and while stirring constantly, cook for 1 minute, or until lightly browned. Stir in the milk, cheese, ketchup, hot sauce, chili powder, paprika, cumin, cayenne, granulated garlic, powdered mustard, and cumin seeds, then while stirring cook until the cheese has melted. Taste and adjust the seasonings, adding salt, if you like.

Transfer the queso to a serving bowl, a small slow cooker, or a chafing dish over a flame and garnish with pickled jalapeño slices. Serve warm with tortilla chips.

1 (14.5-ounce) can diced tomatoes, with juices

1 cup diced yellow onion

2 pounds Velveeta or other brick processed cheese, cubed

8 ounces canned diced green chiles

Tortilla Chips (page 128), for serving

Velveeta was absent from queso recipes until 1939, when the first one appeared in *What'll I Cook?* published by the First Christian Church of Lubbock. Prior to this, most Texan chile con queso recipes used American cheese, which does melt very well but still needs starch to hold the sauce together. On the other hand, Velveeta, which began advertising in Texas in 1930, has fillers that enable it to melt into a smooth sauce without any additional ingredients. Sure, it's more processed than regular American cheese but it's much easier to cook with. It was only a matter of time before queso-loving Texans, such as Mrs. Myron Hinkle who contributed this recipe to the church cookbook, began using it instead of American cheese.

LUBBOCK CHILE CON QUESO

1939 // MAKES ABOUT 16 SERVINGS

In a medium saucepan, combine the tomatoes, onion, cheese, and green chiles. Cook over low heat, stirring occasionally, until the until the cheese has melted and the mixture is well combined.

Transfer the queso to a serving bowl, a small slow cooker, or a chafing dish over a flame. Serve warm with tortilla chips.

2 (10-ounce) cans diced tomatoes with green chiles, with juices

1 cup diced yellow onion

1 clove garlic, minced

¼ cup chili powder

1 tablespoon ground cumin

1 teaspoon dried oregano

1 pound brick processed cheese or aged Cheddar cheese, cubed

1 teaspoon whole milk

Kosher salt

Tortilla Chips (page 128), for serving

This was Lady Bird Johnson's earliest published queso recipe and it ran in the *Washington Post* in 1964, shortly after she became First Lady. The recipe called for aged Cheddar cheese, which is odd since American cheese was the chile con queso standard at the time. When testing the recipe as written, I found that without any dairy or starch to thin and emulsify the sauce, it turned into a disagreeable lump. There was potential, however, as her flavorings, when mixed with Velveeta instead of Cheddar, were quite delicious.

Because later queso recipes attributed to Mrs. Johnson use processed cheese, my assumption is that Cheddar was called for to make the dip seem more sophisticated. The White House chef at the time, René Verdon, had cruelly referred to the Johnson family's favorite appetizer as "chile con concrete," and that descriptor is apt if this dip is made with aged Cheddar instead of processed cheese!

▼△▼△▼△▼△▼△▼△▼△▼△▼△▼△▼△▼△▼△▼△

LADY BIRD JOHNSON'S CHILE CON QUESO

1964 // MAKES 6 TO 8 SERVINGS

In a medium saucepan, stir together the tomatoes, onion, garlic, chili powder, cumin, and oregano. Bring to a boil, turn down the heat to low, and simmer, uncovered, stirring occasionally, until the mixture has reduced to a paste, about 10 minutes. Add the cheese and cook, stirring, until the cheese has melted. If the queso is too thick, thin it with the milk. Taste and add salt if needed.

Transfer the queso to a serving bowl, a small slow cooker, or a chafing dish over a flame. Serve warm with tortilla chips.

TEX-MEX CLASSICS

My first order of business after flying into Dallas from New York was to get a bite to eat. When returning home, some Texans go for barbecue and others go for chicken-fried steak. I'm the type that heads straight for Tex-Mex. When I arrived at the restaurant, two of my dearest friends were already there waiting for me.

As I approached the table, I saw tall glasses of iced tea, a basket of crisp tortilla chips, a small cup of deep-red salsa, and a larger dish full of golden melted cheese speckled with green chiles and topped with a dollop of guacamole—a classic bowl of Tex-Mex queso. "What a treat—I have missed y'all so much!" I said to my friends, sliding into the booth. My dining companions agreed it was wonderful to be together again and we raised our chips and began to eat.

So what exactly is Tex-Mex queso and how does it differ from its brethren along the border? The answer is simple: it is a dip made with processed cheese. There are chiles, of course, but it's the smooth, velvety cheese that provides the foundation. And

although some have been known to spoon it into tortillas or pour it over foods such as steak, Tex-Mex queso's main purpose is to be scooped onto salty chips.

The dish with the name "chile con queso" may have had its beginnings in Mexico, but its most popular form—gooey, molten processed cheese fortified with hot chiles—is more prevalent the farther away you get from the border. Although the two are indeed different, they are still connected, much like a crispy taco in Fort Worth is related to the street taco found in Mexico City. It's like family—you may not look or act like your cousins who live the next state over, but you still share a heritage and a name. You are kin.

When people refer to queso, they're usually talking about Tex-Mex queso. This is the version that managed to become known worldwide. This happened for several reasons. First, it's not difficult to prepare—making a sauce with processed cheese is simple, as the cheese melts easily. Second, Tex-Mex queso is served as a dip, which is a communal, friendly food meant to be shared. And lastly, both chiles and dairy have chemical properties in them that make people feel good, so it's almost therapeutic to eat.

In most homes, Tex-Mex queso is made with a block of processed cheese and a can of spicy tomatoes. Even some restaurants stick to this basic formula. This is a good dish that hits all the right notes, but there is a ton of room for improvisation, which you see throughout the state. For instance, you can liven it up with guacamole and a spoonful of pico de gallo. Proteins such as taco meat, bean dip, or shredded brisket can be stirred into the bowl. And though there is always a base of processed cheese, sometimes it may be white instead of the more familiar yellow, and other cheeses may be added to the mix, as well.

In this chapter, I take you on a tour through some of the more popular Tex-Mex quesos found across the state. (If you are ever at a loss for conversation with a Texan, just ask them about their favorite queso and you'll be gabbing like old friends in no time.) Whether it's queso blanco that's rich with green chiles and favored in the West, the classic bowl of yellow queso topped with Texas red chili enjoyed in the North, the late-night diner-style common in Austin, or a thick and fluffy concoction ubiquitous in Houston, it's all Tex-Mex queso!

FAMOUS TEX-MEX QUESOS

Here are some beloved Tex-Mex restaurant quesos found in Texas.

Bob Armstrong Dip

Named after a former Texas Democratic legislator, this queso came about when Armstrong was eating at Matt's El Rancho in Austin in the late 1960s, and he asked the owner's son, Matt Martinez, to surprise him with something new. Martinez ladled taco meat into a bowl, covered it with queso, then topped it with guacamole and sour cream. A classic queso compuesto was born.

Felix Queso

Felix Tijerina's famous queso has most likely been served in Houston since the 1930s. It is shockingly thick, and a stream of chile-spiked oil flows through the cheese's folds. It may look odd, but those who love it are faithful and true. His restaurant is now closed but Houston's El Patio bought the recipe from the family and continues to offer it today.

The Original José's Dip

Molina is Houston's longest continually open Tex-Mex restaurant, and Jose's Dip is their contribution to the canon of famous Texas quesos. The story goes that decades ago a waiter named José would spoon taco meat into his customers' queso, and thus this addictive queso was named after him.

Kerbey Queso

When I asked people to name their favorite spot to get queso, Austin's Kerbey Lane often got the nod. Theirs is a queso blanco topped with pico de gallo, and most people also add a scoop of guacamole. Because the restaurant is open 24 hours, most associate the queso with fun nights, too.

Magnolia Mud

Magnolia Cafe is another 24-hour Austin diner, and it also serves queso at all hours of the day. Their version is made with yellow cheese and comes topped with pico de gallo. The most popular version they offer, however, is known as Magnolia Mud (Mag Mud, for those in the know), which includes black beans and guacamole.

¼ cup vegetable oil

¼ cup diced yellow onion

¾ cup diced grape tomatoes

1 clove garlic, minced

1 teaspoon chili powder

1 teaspoon paprika

¼ teaspoon kosher salt

¼ teaspoon cayenne

¼ cup all-purpose flour

¼ cup water

8 ounces yellow American cheese, shredded

Tortilla Chips (page 128), for serving

Felix Tijerina was a chile con queso pioneer. A longstanding Houston restaurateur, he opened his second restaurant in 1937, which he gave his own name. It grew into a beloved local chain, but the last location closed in 2008. His menu was composed of Tex-Mex classics, such as cheese enchiladas and crispy tacos, but it was his distinctive queso, thick and oozing with red grease, that stood apart from the rest. It looked frightening but was surprisingly fluffy and addictive.

This version is an amalgamation of several recipes that appeared in Houston publications over the years. Although purists may scoff that it's not entirely accurate, the slick of chile-spiced oil pooled on a thick pillow of melted cheese is present and deliciously unique.

▼△▼△▼△▼△▼△▼△▼△▼△▼△▼△

FELIX QUESO

MAKES 4 TO 6 SERVINGS

In a medium saucepan, warm the oil over low heat. Add the onion, tomatoes, garlic, chili powder, paprika, salt, and cayenne and cook, stirring occasionally, until the tomatoes have almost completely disintegrated, 6 to 8 minutes.

Whisk together the flour and the water to make a paste, then add it to the pan. Stir a few times until the paste is well combined with the vegetables. Stirring constantly, add the cheese, which should combine quickly. As the cheese melts, the queso will become thick and almost like putty. Don't be alarmed! This is the proper texture as it is not a creamy queso. Taste and adjust the seasonings, if you like.

Transfer the queso to a serving bowl, a small slow cooker, or a chafing dish over a flame. Serve immediately with tortilla chips.

2 tablespoons unsalted butter

¼ cup diced yellow onion

4 jalapeños, seeded and finely diced

2 cloves garlic, minced

2 Anaheim chiles, roasted (see page 3), peeled, seeded, and finely diced

2 tablespoons cornstarch

1 cup whole milk

1 cup water

1 pound white or yellow American cheese, shredded

2 tablespoons chopped fresh cilantro

1 teaspoon ground cumin

¼ teaspoon cayenne

½ teaspoon kosher salt

Guacamole (page 125), for topping

Pico de Gallo (page 125), for topping

Tortilla Chips (page 128), for serving

In Richard Linklater's film *Boyhood,* the protagonist finds himself in an Austin diner with his girlfriend late one night. They are being philosophical, and when she asks what they are doing there at three o'clock in the morning, he replies, "You know what we're doing here? Queso!" In Austin, inviting places such as Kerbey Lane and Magnolia Cafe have long been popular spots for people to get their queso fix in the darker hours. This recipe is not specific to any particular place, but will remind you of late nights and good friends.

▽△▽△▽△▽△▽△▽△▽△▽△▽△▽△▽△

AUSTIN DINER-STYLE QUESO
MAKES 6 TO 8 SERVINGS

In a medium saucepan, melt the butter over medium-low heat. Add the onion and jalapeños and cook, stirring occasionally, until softened, about 5 minutes. Add the garlic and Anaheims and cook for 30 seconds longer.

Whisk together the cornstarch, milk, and water until well combined, then pour into the pan. Bring to a simmer, stirring constantly, and cook for a couple of minutes until the mixture begins to thicken. Add the cheese, turn down the heat to low, and cook, stirring, until the cheese has melted. Stir in the cilantro, cumin, cayenne, and salt, then taste and adjust the seasonings, if you like.

Transfer the queso to a serving bowl, a small slow cooker, or a chafing dish over a flame. Spoon guacamole and pico de gallo into the center of the queso. Serve warm with tortilla chips.

MAG MUD-STYLE QUESO
Stir in 1 cup cooked, drained black beans before adding guacamole and pico de gallo. (For information about the name, see page 29.)

FIERY RED SALSA

1 red bell pepper, halved lengthwise and seeded

4 habanero chiles, preferably red, halved lengthwise and seeded

¼ medium yellow onion

2 cloves garlic, peeled

1 (8-ounce) can tomato sauce

½ cup vegetable oil

1 tablespoon white vinegar

¼ teaspoon ground cumin

Kosher salt

QUESO

1 cup Green Chile Salsa Verde (page 126)

1 pound brick processed cheese, cubed

Kosher salt

Guacamole (page 125), for topping

1 ounce crumbled queso fresco or feta cheese

Chopped fresh cilantro, for garnish

Tortilla Chips (page 128), for serving

Many consider the queso at the Austin-based chain Torchy's Tacos among the finest in Texas. It's a recipe much in demand, but the one the restaurant has shared tastes nothing like what they serve. Then one day I came across a copycat version of its habanero salsa, which I realized is the key to the queso's distinctive flavor. After tweaking that recipe, I was able to craft a queso that's very close. I've named it after the restaurant's catchphrase, and the name fits!

DAMN GOOD QUESO

MAKES 6 TO 8 SERVINGS

To make the salsa, position a rack 6 inches from the upper heating element and preheat the broiler. Line a baking sheet with aluminum foil. Place the bell pepper and habaneros on the baking sheet skin-side up, then add the onion and garlic. Broil for 2 minutes. Remove the baking sheet from the oven; the habaneros should be slightly darkened and fragrant. Transfer the habaneros to a blender. Return the baking sheet to the oven and broil for 3 to 5 minutes longer, or until everything is beginning to blacken. Place the onion, garlic, tomato sauce, oil, vinegar, and cumin in the blender. When the bell pepper is cool enough to handle, gently pull away the blackened skin and discard, then add the bell pepper to the blender, too. Blend until smooth. Add salt to taste. Pour the salsa into a jar or other storage container. (The salsa will keep, refrigerated, for 1 week—it goes well with most anything!)

CONTINUED

To make the queso, pour the green chile salsa into a medium saucepan and add the cheese. Cook over low heat, stirring occasionally, until the cheese has melted. Taste and add salt, if you like.

Transfer the queso to a serving bowl, a small slow cooker, or a chafing dish over a flame. Spoon the guacamole into the center of the queso, drizzle with fiery salsa, and garnish with the cheese and cilantro. Serve warm with tortilla chips.

MIND THE CHEESE, PLEASE

Remember: In recipes calling for processed cheese, **brick processed cheese** is what most people know as Velveeta where as **American Cheese** is a processed cheese that can be purchased by the pound from the deli counter (which is what I recommend) or in packages of individually wrapped slices. They are two different cheeses and should be treated as such! (See page 7 for more information.)

1 tablespoon unsalted butter

¼ cup diced yellow onion

2 tablespoons cornstarch

1 cup whole milk

1 cup water

8 ounces white American cheese, shredded

4 ounces Monterey Jack cheese, shredded

4 ounces white Cheddar cheese, shredded

½ teaspoon ground cumin

¼ teaspoon cayenne

4 Anaheim chiles, roasted (see page 3), peeled, seeded, and finely diced

2 to 4 jalapeños, roasted (see page 3), peeled, seeded, and finely diced

½ teaspoon kosher salt

Tortilla Chips (page 128), for serving

In the area of West Texas close to the Permian Basin and the Panhandle, chile con queso made with white cheese and long green chiles is the main style. Cheeses such as Monterey Jack and white Cheddar may be included in the base, but white American cheese provides the foundation, which not only helps the queso stay smooth but also gives it that distinct North of the Border taste. Here is my take on this style, which is sometimes called queso blanco. You can make this recipe either mild or spicy, depending on the heat of your chiles and how many jalapeños you use. It is only lightly seasoned with ground cumin and a hit of cayenne, so the dominant flavor is of the roasted chiles and cheese.

WEST TEXAS GREEN CHILE QUESO BLANCO

MAKES 6 TO 8 SERVINGS

In a medium saucepan, melt the butter over medium-low heat. Add the onion and cook, stirring occasionally, until softened, about 5 minutes.

Whisk together the cornstarch, milk, and water until well combined, then pour into the pan. Bring to a simmer, stirring constantly, and cook for a couple of minutes, until the mixture begins to thicken. Add the American cheese, turn down the heat to low, and cook, stirring, until the cheese has melted. One handful at a time, add the Monterey Jack and Cheddar cheeses, stirring until melted before adding more. When the mixture is smooth, stir in the cumin, cayenne, Anaheims, jalapeños, and salt. Taste and adjust the seasonings, if you like.

Transfer the queso to a serving bowl, a slow cooker, or a chafing dish over a flame. Serve warm with tortilla chips.

1 tablespoon
unsalted butter

2 cloves garlic, minced

1 cup chopped fresh
baby spinach

½ teaspoon kosher salt

¼ teaspoon cayenne

2 tablespoons
cornstarch

1 cup whole milk

1 cup water

1 pound white American
cheese, shredded

4 Anaheim chiles,
roasted (see page 3),
peeled, seeded, and
diced

Pico de Gallo (page 125),
for topping

1 avocado, halved, pitted,
peeled, and sliced

Tortilla Chips (page 128),
for serving

In Texas, we like to put spinach in our queso when we're feeling healthy. This version is inspired by the spinach queso found at one of the state's oldest restaurants, The Original in Fort Worth. If you're looking to increase your fill of vegetables, this may become your favorite thing to eat.

▼▲▼▲▼▲▼▲▼▲▼▲▼▲▼▲▼▲▼▲▼

SPINACH QUESO BLANCO

MAKES 6 TO 8 SERVINGS

In a medium saucepan, melt the butter over medium-low heat. Add the garlic and cook for 30 seconds. Add the spinach and cook, stirring occasionally, until wilted, about 5 minutes. Season with the salt and cayenne, then drain the spinach in a colander.

Rinse and wipe out the saucepan, then add the cornstarch, milk, and water and whisk until well combined. Bring to a simmer over medium-low heat, stirring constantly, and cook for a couple of minutes, until the mixture begins to thicken. Add the cheese, turn down the heat to low, and cook, stirring, until the cheese has melted. Stir in the spinach and Anaheims. Taste and adjust the seasonings, if you like.

Transfer the queso to a serving bowl, a small slow cooker, or a chafing dish over a flame. Top with the pico de gallo and sliced avocado. Serve warm with tortilla chips.

SPINACH-ARTICHOKE QUESO
Stir in 1 cup chopped artichoke hearts before topping with the pico de gallo and avocado.

BACON-SPINACH QUESO
Stir in 8 slices cooked and crumbled bacon and ½ teaspoon smoked paprika before topping with the pico de gallo and avocado.

2 tablespoons
unsalted butter

¼ cup diced yellow onion

½ cup finely diced
jarred cactus, rinsed

2 cloves garlic, minced

¾ cup fresh or thawed
frozen corn kernels

2 tablespoons
cornstarch

1 cup whole milk

1 cup water

½ pound white American
cheese, shredded

½ pound Monterey
Jack cheese, shredded

2 poblano chiles, roasted
(see page 3), peeled,
seeded, and diced

1 teaspoon ground
cumin

½ teaspoon kosher salt

¼ teaspoon cayenne

¼ cup chopped fresh
cilantro

Tortilla Chips (page 128),
for serving

Cactus grows abundantly in Texas and it's a popular vegetable in South Texas. If you've never had it, it's refreshingly vegetal and crunchy, sort of like a cross between okra and green beans. It can be steamed, sauteed, and roasted, but when it comes to including it in queso, I prefer to use the jarred and pickled variety. Not only is it easier to prepare (you don't have to worry about removing those pesky needles), but it's also tangy—a perfect foil to the rich cheese. (Jarred cactus can be ordered online from mexgrocer.com.) This recipe also includes sweet corn and earthy poblano chiles, making this mild yet flavorful queso a South Texas treat.

CACTUS & CORN QUESO POBLANO

MAKES 6 TO 8 SERVINGS

In a medium saucepan, melt the butter over medium-low heat. Add the onion and cactus and cook, stirring occasionally, until softened, about 5 minutes. Add the garlic and corn and cook for 2 minutes longer.

Whisk together the cornstarch, milk, and water until well combined, then pour into the pan. Bring to a simmer, stirring constantly, and cook for a couple of minutes, until the mixture begins to thicken. Add the American cheese, turn down the heat to low, and cook, stirring, until the cheese has melted. Add a handful of the Monterey Jack, stirring until melted before adding another handful, and repeat until all of the cheese has been used. Stir in the poblanos, cumin, salt, and cayenne, then taste and adjust the seasonings, if you like.

Transfer the queso to a serving bowl, a small slow cooker, or a chafing dish over a flame. Garnish with the cilantro. Serve warm with tortilla chips.

2 cups cooked drained pinto beans or 1 (15-ounce) can pinto beans, drained

2 cloves garlic, minced

¼ cup Pickled Jalapeños (page 126), plus more for garnish

2 tablespoons liquid from Pickled Jalapeños (page 126)

1 teaspoon chili powder

Kosher salt

2 tablespoons unsalted butter

¼ cup diced onion

2 fresh jalapeños, seeded and diced

2 tablespoons cornstarch

1 cup whole milk

1 cup water

1 pound yellow American cheese, shredded

½ teaspoon ground cumin

Tortilla Chips (page 128), for serving

Willie Nelson once sang, "My blood type is queso." Mine, however, would probably be refried beans. As a matter of fact, when I first moved to New York, decent refried beans were not served anywhere, and it was my obsession with them that prompted me to learn how to cook all the Tex-Mex classics. If you mix refried beans with pickled jalapeños, pickle juice, and chili powder, you get a tangy dip that is a natural partner to salty corn chips. And if you add a scoop of this bean dip to a bowl of hot, creamy queso, you will have fuel for life indeed.

▼△▼△▼△▼△▼△▼△▼△▼△▼△▼△▼△

BEAN DIP QUESO

MAKES 6 TO 8 SERVINGS

Place the beans, garlic, pickled jalapeños, jalapeño juice, and chili powder in a blender. Puree until smooth and add salt to taste.

In a medium saucepan, melt the butter over medium-low heat. Add the onion and diced jalapeños and cook, stirring occasionally, until softened, about 5 minutes.

Whisk together the cornstarch, milk, and water until well combined and pour into the pan. Bring to a simmer, stirring constantly, and cook for a couple of minutes, until the mixture begins to thicken. Add the cheese, turn down the heat to low, and cook, stirring, until the cheese has melted. Stir in the cumin, then taste and adjust seasonings, adding salt if you like.

Transfer the queso to a serving bowl, a small slow cooker, or a chafing dish over a flame. Spoon the bean dip into the center of the queso, then garnish with pickled jalapeño slices. Serve warm with tortilla chips.

PULLED PORK

1 pound boneless pork shoulder, cut into 4 chunks

½ teaspoon kosher salt

¾ cup Green Chile Salsa Verde (page 126)

¼ cup water

1 tablespoon fresh lime juice

QUESO

2 tablespoons cornstarch

1 cup whole milk

1 cup water

1 pound white American cheese, shredded

¼ cup Green Chile Salsa Verde (page 126)

1 teaspoon ground cumin

¼ teaspoon cayenne

2 poblano chiles, roasted (see page 3), peeled, stemmed, seeded, and diced

Pickled Jalapeños (page 126), for topping

1 avocado, halved, pitted, peeled, and diced

Tortilla Chips (page 128), for serving

Pulled pork is not the most iconic Texan dish but it's a popular one and is a hearty addition to queso. For mine, I simmer pork shoulder in salsa verde, then make a queso blanco riddled with poblano chiles. After adding the shredded pork to the queso, I garnish with pickled jalapeños and diced avocado to balance out the meat and cheese.

▼▲▼▲▼▲▼▲▼▲▼▲▼▲▼▲▼▲▼▲▼▲▼▲▼

QUESO BLANCO WITH GREEN CHILE PULLED PORK

MAKES 6 TO 8 SERVINGS

To make the pulled pork, preheat the oven to 275°F.

Place the pork in a Dutch oven and sprinkle it with the salt. Add the green chile salsa verde and water. Cover the pot and place in the oven. Cook for 2 hours, or until the pork shreds easily when pulled apart with a fork. Alternatively, place the pork and salsa verde in a slow cooker and cook on low for 6 hours. When the pork is done, shred it with a fork and stir in the lime juice. Taste and adjust the seasonings, if you like.

To make the queso, in a medium saucepan, whisk together the cornstarch, milk, and water. Bring to a simmer over medium-low heat, stirring constantly, and cook for a couple of minutes, until thickened. Add the cheese, turn down the heat to low, and cook, stirring, until the cheese has melted. Stir in the salsa verde, cumin, cayenne, and diced poblanos. Taste and adjust the seasonings, adding salt if you like.

Transfer the queso to a serving bowl, a small slow cooker, or a chafing dish over a flame. Spoon the pulled pork into the center of the queso and top with pickled jalapeños and avocado. Serve warm with tortilla chips.

CHILI

1 teaspoon bacon grease or vegetable oil

¼ medium yellow onion, chopped

2 cloves garlic, chopped

2 ounces dried ancho chiles, seeded and rehydrated (see page 4)

½ (10-ounce) can diced tomatoes with green chiles, with juices

1 teaspoon dried oregano

1 teaspoon ground cumin

Pinch of ground allspice

Pinch of cayenne

1½ cups water

1 pound ground beef, preferably coarsely ground

½ teaspoon kosher salt

½ teaspoon black pepper

QUESO

1 pound brick processed cheese, cubed

½ (10-ounce) can diced tomatoes with green chiles, with juices

¼ cup Pickled Jalapeños (page 126)

¼ cup diced yellow onion

Tortilla Chips (page 128), for serving

Chili parlors may no longer be ubiquitous in Texas, but spots such as the Texas Chili Parlor in Austin and La Familia in Fort Worth still offer a bowl of Texas red and often pair it with queso. President Lyndon Baines Johnson was said to be fond of this combination, so the chili here is a riff on his family's recipe, though instead of using chili powder I call for dried ancho chiles, which makes for a richer and more flavorful stew.

▽▲▽▲▽▲▽▲▽▲▽▲▽▲▽▲▽▲▽▲▽

CHILI PARLOR QUESO

MAKES 6 TO 8 SERVINGS

To make the chili, in a medium saucepan, warm the bacon grease over medium-low heat. Add the onion and cook, stirring occasionally, until softened, about 5 minutes. Add the garlic and cook for 30 seconds longer. Turn off the heat. Transfer the onion and garlic to a blender. Add the anchos, tomatoes, oregano, cumin, allspice, cayenne, and water. Blend until smooth.

Add the ground beef to the pan and season it with the salt and black pepper. Cook over medium-low heat, stirring occasionally, until browned, about 10 minutes. Pour in the chile puree. Turn the heat to high, bring the mixture to a boil, then turn down the heat and simmer, uncovered, for 30 to 45 minutes, stirring occasionally, until thickened and fragrant. If the chili gets too dry, add more water. Taste and adjust the seasonings, if you like.

To make the queso, in another medium saucepan, combine the cheese and tomatoes. Cook over low heat, stirring occasionally, until the cheese has melted.

Transfer the queso to a serving bowl, a slow cooker, or a chafing dish over a flame. Spoon the chili into the center of the queso and top with the pickled jalapeños and onion. Serve warm with tortilla chips.

PICADILLO

½ pound ground beef

¼ cup diced yellow onion

2 cloves garlic, minced

1 tablespoon chili powder

½ teaspoon ground cumin

½ teaspoon dried oregano

½ teaspoon kosher salt

QUESO

2 tablespoons unsalted butter

¼ cup diced yellow onion

4 jalapeños, seeded and finely diced

2 tablespoons cornstarch

2 cloves garlic, minced

2 cups chicken broth

1 pound yellow American cheese, shredded

1 teaspoon ground cumin

½ teaspoon kosher salt

¼ teaspoon cayenne

Pico de Gallo (page 125), for topping

Tortilla Chips (page 128), for serving

Queso compuesto is a queso with additional ingredients added to the creamy base, such as guacamole, beans, or meat. There are many variations on this theme but stirring in a scoop of picadillo, also known as taco meat, may just be the most popular one of all.

▼▲▽▲▽▲▽▲▽▲▽▲▽▲▽▲▽▲▽▲▽▲

QUESO WITH BEEF PICADILLO

MAKES 6 TO 8 SERVINGS

To make the picadillo, heat a large skillet over medium-low heat. Add the beef and onion and cook, stirring occasionally, until the meat is lightly browned, about 10 minutes. Stir in the garlic, chili powder, cumin, oregano, and salt and continue to cook until the meat is well done, about 5 minutes longer. Taste and adjust the seasonings, if you like. Drain any excess grease from the picadillo.

To make the queso, in a medium saucepan, melt the butter over medium-low heat. Add the onion and jalapeños and cook until softened, about 5 minutes. Add the garlic and cook for 30 seconds longer.

Whisk together the cornstarch and chicken broth until well combined, then pour into the pan. Bring to a simmer, stirring constantly, and cook for a couple of minutes, until the mixture begins to thicken. Add the cheese, turn down the heat to low, and cook, stirring, until the cheese has melted. Stir in the cumin, salt, and cayenne, then taste and adjust the seasonings, if you like.

CONTINUED

Transfer the queso to a serving bowl, a small slow cooker, or a chafing dish over a flame. Spoon the picadillo into the center of the queso, then top with pico de gallo. Serve warm with tortilla chips.

BOB ARMSTRONG–STYLE QUESO
When ready to serve, add guacamole (page 125) and sour cream to the queso. (For information about the name, see page 29.)

TAILGATE-STYLE QUESO
Swap out the picadillo for 1 pound breakfast sausage, cooked and drained.

3 canned chipotle chiles in adobo sauce

2 tablespoons fresh cilantro

2 cloves garlic

¼ cup fresh lime juice

¼ cup olive oil

1 teaspoon kosher salt

½ teaspoon black pepper

½ teaspoon ground cumin

1 pound skirt steak

2 tablespoons unsalted butter

¼ cup diced yellow onion

2 jalapeños, seeded and diced

2 tablespoons cornstarch

1 cup half-and-half

1 cup water

1 pound yellow American cheese, shredded

Guacamole (page 125), for topping

Pico de Gallo (page 125), for topping

Tortilla Chips (page 128), for serving

Grilled skirt steak folded into tortillas is known as fajitas. Originating in northern Mexico, fajita steak, which rose to popularity in Houston in the 1970s, also makes for a good addition to a bowl of melted cheese. For this version, I use a smoky bright marinade made from chipotle chiles and lime juice, and I quickly cook the steak under the broiler—but it could easily be prepared on the grill instead.

▽△▽△▽△▽△▽△▽△▽△▽△▽△▽△▽△▽△

CHIPOTLE BEEF FAJITA QUESO

MAKES 6 TO 8 SERVINGS

Place the chipotles, cilantro, garlic, lime juice, olive oil, salt, black pepper, and cumin in a blender or food processor and blend until smooth to make a marinade. Reserve 1 tablespoon for the queso.

Place the steak in a bowl and add the rest of the marinade. Cover and refrigerate for 1 to 2 hours, turning the steak a couple of times. (Don't marinate longer than 2 hours or the texture will begin to get mushy.)

While the steak is marinating, in a medium saucepan, warm the butter with the reserved 1 tablespoon marinade over medium-low heat. Add the onion and jalapeños and cook, stirring occasionally, until softened, about 5 minutes. Whisk together the cornstarch, half-and-half, and water until well combined, then pour into the pan. Bring to a simmer, stirring constantly, and cook for a couple of minutes, until the mixture begins to thicken. Add the cheese, turn down the heat to low, and cook, stirring, until the cheese has melted. Add salt to taste. Cover and turn off the heat.

CONTINUED

After the steak has marinated, position a rack about 4 inches from the upper heating element and place a large, broiler-safe skillet on the rack. Preheat the broiler and skillet for 10 minutes.

With a paper towel, wipe the marinade from the steak, pat the steak dry, and cut it in half so it will fit in the skillet. Carefully remove the hot skillet from the oven and lay the steak in the skillet. Broil the steak, turning once, until nicely charred on both sides, 6 to 8 minutes for medium-rare or 10 to 12 minutes for medium. Transfer the steak to a cutting board, cover, and let rest for 10 minutes. Meanwhile, reheat the queso over low heat, stirring occasionally.

Slice the steak against the grain, then cut the slices into ½-inch cubes. Transfer the queso to a serving bowl, a small slow cooker, or a chafing dish over a flame. Top the queso with the steak and spoon on guacamole and pico de gallo. Serve warm with tortilla chips.

BRISKET

1 (14.5-ounce) can diced tomatoes, preferably fire-roasted, with juices

4 canned chipotle chiles in adobo sauce

2 cloves garlic

¼ cup fresh cilantro

½ teaspoon ground cumin

Kosher salt

Black pepper

1 (12-ounce) bottle dark beer, such as Shiner Bock (see note)

1 pound flat-cut beef brisket (see Note)

QUESO

1 tablespoon unsalted butter

¼ cup diced yellow onion

1 pound brick processed cheese, cubed

Pico de Gallo (page 125), for topping

Tortilla Chips (page 128), for serving

Queso with brisket is plentiful across Texas. Sometimes barbecue joints will throw a few smoky ends into a bowl, but more often the brisket is slowly braised until tender and juicy. This brisket queso falls into the latter camp, with the meat simmered in a savory bath of ranchero salsa and the dark Texas beer Shiner Bock, which gives it a particularly Texan taste.

▽△▽△▽△▽△▽△▽△▽△▽△▽△▽△▽△▽△▽△

BRISKET QUESO
MAKES 6 TO 8 SERVINGS

To prepare the brisket, preheat the oven to 275°F.

Place the diced tomatoes, chipotles, garlic, cilantro, cumin, ¼ teaspoon salt, and ¼ teaspoon black pepper in a blender. Blend until smooth. Stir in the beer. Taste and adjust the seasonings, if you like. Measure out 1 cup of the mixture, cover, and refrigerate until needed.

Place the brisket in a 3-quart Dutch oven. Season it with salt and pepper and add the remaining tomato-beer mixture. Cover the pot and place in the oven. Cook until the brisket shreds easily when pulled apart with a fork, about 4 hours. Alternatively, place the brisket and tomato-beer mixture in a slow cooker and cook on low for 6 hours. When the brisket is done, shred it with a fork and mix with the pan juices.

To make the queso, in a medium saucepan, melt the butter over medium-low heat. Add the onion and cook, stirring occasionally, until softened, about 5 minutes. Pour in the reserved beer-tomato mixture and add the cheese. Cook on low, stirring occasionally, until the cheese has melted. Taste and adjust the seasonings, if you like.

Transfer the queso to a serving bowl, a small slow cooker, or a chafing dish over a flame. Place the shredded brisket in the center of the queso (the brisket will probably sink!) and top with pico de gallo. Serve warm with tortilla chips.

NOTE: If brisket is unavailable, you can substitute chuck roast, shoulder steak, or boneless short ribs. Negro Modelo is a good substitute for Shiner Bock.

ON THE BORDER

When I realized I had left my credit card at Chope's, a restaurant in the southern New Mexican town of La Mesa, I called and spoke to the manager, Jennifer Holguin, to see if it was still there. She assured me that it was and so instead of heading deeper into New Mexico, I returned to the roadside spot not far from El Paso in the Mesilla Valley along the Rio Grande. It was a beautiful drive; shade trees lined the road, fields were lush with green chile plants in bloom, and in the distance, craggy mountains rose into the wide blue sky.

Jennifer had told me to meet her in the kitchen, so I walked around to the back of the restaurant and she came out to greet me with my credit card. I thanked her, and then while I had her attention, asked about her chile con queso, which I'd had earlier at lunch. "So, you put meat in your chile con queso," I began, but she quickly shook her head.

"There's no meat," she said. I described what I had eaten and she realized I'd had green chili, a stew made with peppers and beef, which had been topped with a thick blanket of melted cheese. I ordered the wrong thing and since I didn't know any better, I just assumed that was the southern New Mexican queso style.

She apologized for the confusion and then walked to the stove, grabbed a cup, and threw in a handful of shredded white cheese. "Now, this is how we make our chile con queso," she said as she ladled a green chile salsa simmering on the stove into the cup before topping it with more shredded white cheese. The cheese melted into the warm salsa and created a blend that was supple enough to be eaten with chips, but a stack of tortillas would be just as welcome to sop up the verdant queso. It was delicious and I thanked her for her hospitality.

Because the exact origins of chile con queso are unknown, I decided its spiritual birthplace was in the area today referred to as "the Borderplex," which encompasses southern New Mexico, El Paso, and its sister city Juarez across the border in Chihuahua, Mexico. Not only is Chihuahua the state where chile con queso is most prominent in Mexico, but the region is also where Spanish explorers first arrived in that part of the world with dairy-producing livestock and where native long green chiles grow abundantly.

From there, I began my exploration of chile con queso along the border, following the Rio Grande from southern New Mexico all the way to the Gulf of Mexico. Along the way, I was surprised to see the regional variations in chile con queso, with distinctive queso styles appearing sometimes just a few miles from the previous. For instance, in El Paso, chile con queso was a mound of green chile strips nestled in a soft blanket of white cheese. In Canutillo, queso makers eschewed the white cheese common to the area and proudly used Velveeta instead. In Laredo, a chewy, thick queso studded with tangy sausage was the standard. Closer to the ocean, there were skillet quesos topped with fresh shrimp.

For someone like me who has only had melted yellow chile con queso, the array along the border was an eye-opening adventure. Here are some of the variations I found, which makes it possible to explore the diversity in your kitchen at home, too.

1 tablespoon vegetable oil

1 cup diced yellow onion

2 cloves garlic, minced

2 cups water

½ teaspoon kosher salt

¼ teaspoon ground cumin

6 Anaheim chiles, roasted (see page 3), peeled, seeded, and chopped

8 ounces mild white Cheddar cheese, shredded

Tortilla Chips (page 128) and/or warm corn or flour tortillas, for serving

This is similar to the chile con queso served at Chope's in Mesilla, New Mexico. It's a classic New Mexican stewed green chile salsa with handfuls of shredded white cheese added right before serving. It's not a thick and creamy queso but instead a bit soupy, and to someone who hasn't had this style before, it may seem unusual. But that doesn't detract from its deep chile flavor that goes well with both tortillas and chips.

▼△▼△▼△▼△▼△▼△▼△▼△▼△▼△▼△▼

SOUTHERN NEW MEXICO CHILE CON QUESO

MAKES 4 TO 6 SERVINGS

In a medium saucepan, warm the vegetable oil over medium-low heat. Add the onion and cook, stirring occasionally, until softened, about 5 minutes. Add the garlic and cook for 30 seconds longer. Add the water, salt, cumin, and Anaheims to the pan and turn down the heat to low. Cook, stirring occasionally, for 30 minutes, or until everything has softened. Turn off the heat and, with a potato masher or the back of a wooden spoon, mash everything together until a thick sauce forms. Taste and adjust the seasonings, if you like.

Sprinkle the cheese over the salsa and continue to cook, without stirring, until melted, a couple of minutes.

Serve warm in bowls, with tortilla chips and/or warm tortillas.

1 tablespoon
unsalted butter

¼ cup diced
yellow onion

2 Anaheim chiles,
roasted (see page 3),
peeled, seeded, and
diced

4 jalapeños, roasted
(see page 3), seeded,
and diced

1 cup sour cream

8 ounces Muenster
cheese, shredded

¼ teaspoon kosher salt

Tortilla Chips
(page 128) and/or
warm flour tortillas,
for serving

On my drive from El Paso to Marfa, Texas, I stopped at
Tortilleria Lizy, a warm and inviting restaurant in the town
of Van Horn. I ordered the queso, of course, and as I dipped
into it, I noticed that even though it wasn't made with
processed cheese, it was creamier than what I'd had back
in El Paso. There was a bit of tang to it, as well.

I asked the waitress for the recipe and she shared it with
me (her mother was both the cook and the owner). As I
suspected, sour cream is stirred into the mixture, which not
only lends that distinctive flavor but also holds the queso
together. What a happy discovery!

VAN HORN CHILE CON QUESO

MAKES 6 TO 8 SERVINGS

In a medium saucepan, melt the butter over medium-low heat.
Add the onion and cook, stirring occasionally, until softened,
about 5 minutes.

Add the Anaheims, jalapeños, and sour cream to the pan. Stir
until well combined. Add the cheese and cook, stirring, until
melted, about 2 minutes. Stir in the salt, then taste and adjust
the seasonings, if you like.

Transfer the queso to a serving bowl, a small slow cooker, or a chafing
dish over a flame. Serve warm with tortilla chips and/or tortillas.

1 tablespoon unsalted butter

¼ medium yellow onion, finely diced

2 cloves garlic, minced

¼ cup whole milk

8 ounces brick processed cheese, cubed

8 ounces Monterey Jack cheese, shredded

¼ teaspoon kosher salt

¼ teaspoon ground cumin

¼ teaspoon cayenne

8 Anaheim chiles, roasted (see page 3), peeled, seeded, and chopped

Tortilla Chips (page 128), for serving

After spending a few days eating chile con queso in El Paso and southern New Mexico, when I stopped at the Little Diner in the neighboring town of Canutillo, Texas, I expected much of the same thing—a white queso rich with chiles. The waitress brought me my bowl and though there was indeed lots of chiles in the queso, I noticed the cheese was yellow and ultrasmooth. "Is this . . ." I began to ask, but before I had a chance to finish she smiled and said, "Yes, it's Velveeta." Indeed, other restaurants in Canutillo use brick processed cheese instead of the white cheese, too.

▼▲▼▲▼▲▼▲▼▲▼▲▼▲▼▲▼▲▼▲▼▲

CANUTILLO CHILE CON QUESO

MAKES 6 TO 8 SERVINGS

In a medium saucepan, melt the butter over medium-low heat. Add the onion and cook, stirring occasionally, until softened, about 5 minutes. Add the garlic and cook for 30 seconds longer. Turn down the heat to low. Add the milk, processed cheese, Monterey Jack cheese, salt, cumin, and cayenne. Cook, stirring occasionally, until the cheese has melted. Stir in the Anaheims. Taste and adjust the seasonings, if you like.

Transfer the queso to a serving bowl, a small slow cooker, or a chafing dish over a flame. Serve warm with tortilla chips.

1 tablespoon unsalted butter

¼ medium yellow onion, thinly sliced

¾ cup diced grape tomatoes

2 cloves garlic, minced

6 poblano chiles, roasted (see page 3), peeled, seeded, and cut into 2-inch strips

3 tablespoons heavy cream

1 pound Muenster or Monterey Jack cheese, shredded

¼ teaspoon kosher salt

¼ teaspoon ground cumin

Tortilla Chips (page 128) and/or warm flour tortillas, for serving

"Be sure and try the chile con queso," said a friend when I told her I was visiting El Paso. "It's not like anything you've ever eaten." It's true, the chile con queso in this West Texas border town is more Mexican than Texan, as the strings of white cheese and thick strips of roasted green chiles call for tortillas rather than chips, though people eat it with both. It's enjoyed as both an appetizer and a side dish, and it's often seen smothered on top of eggs, steaks, and fries, too.

EL PASO CHILE CON QUESO

MAKES 6 TO 8 SERVINGS

In a large skillet, melt the butter over medium-low heat. Add the onion and cook, stirring occasionally, until softened, about 5 minutes. Add the tomatoes and garlic and cook for 30 seconds longer. Stir in the poblanos, cream, and cheese and cook, stirring occasionally, until the cheese has melted. Stir in the salt and cumin, then taste and adjust the seasonings, if you like.

Transfer the queso to a serving bowl, a small slow cooker, or a chafing dish over a flame. Serve with tortilla chips and/or warm tortillas.

2 ancho chiles, seeded, rehydrated (see page 4), and chopped

2 tablespoons red wine vinegar

¼ cup water

2 tablespoons chopped yellow onion

1 clove garlic, chopped

½ teaspoon kosher salt

½ teaspoon ground cumin

½ teaspoon paprika

½ teaspoon dried oregano

¼ teaspoon ground cinnamon

¼ teaspoon cayenne

1 tablespoon vegetable oil

½ pound ground pork

1 pound Monterey Jack cheese, shredded

Warm flour tortillas, for serving

In the South Texas border town of Laredo, a skillet queso of stringy white cheese studded with tangy chorizo sausage reigns supreme. *Choriqueso,* as it's commonly known, is so prevalent that it can be difficult to find creamy yellow queso there. This is a hearty dish meant to be eaten with tortillas, and it can be enjoyed at any hour of the day. You could use store-bought chorizo and remove the casing, but it's not difficult to make your own, as many in Laredo do and as I do here.

▽△▽△▽△▽△▽△▽△▽△▽△▽△▽△▽△

CHORIQUESO

MAKES 6 TO 8 SERVINGS

Place the anchos in a blender with the vinegar and water. Blend until smooth, then add the onion, garlic, salt, cumin, paprika, oregano, cinnamon, and cayenne. Blend again until smooth, scraping down the sides with a rubber spatula as needed. If it's too stiff to blend properly, add water, 1 tablespoon at a time.

In a large broiler-safe skillet, warm the vegetable oil over medium-low heat. Pour in the chile puree and cook for 1 minute. Add the ground pork and stir until well combined with the sauce. Cook, stirring occasionally, until no longer pink, about 10 minutes. Taste and adjust the seasonings, if you like.

Position a rack 6 inches from the upper heating element and preheat the broiler.

Evenly sprinkle the Monterey Jack cheese over the cooked chorizo in the skillet. Place the skillet under the broiler and cook for 2 minutes, or until the cheese is lightly browned and bubbling.

Serve warm in the skillet with tortillas.

2 tablespoons
unsalted butter

½ medium yellow onion,
thinly sliced

2 cups fresh or thawed
frozen corn kernels

2 cloves garlic, minced

6 poblano chiles,
roasted (see page 3),
peeled, seeded, and cut
into thin 2-inch-long
strips

½ cup heavy cream

½ cup sour cream

2 tablespoons chopped
fresh cilantro, plus more
for garnish

½ teaspoon dried
oregano

½ teaspoon kosher salt

8 ounces Monterey Jack
cheese, shredded

1 teaspoon fresh lime
juice

1 ounce cotija or feta
cheese, crumbled

Warm corn or flour
tortillas, for serving
(optional)

In this dish, strips of roasted poblano chiles hang out in a creamy sauce with tender kernels of sweet corn. It's typically served as a side dish in Mexico but it can also be nestled in tortillas or served with tortilla chips, too.

RAJAS Y ELOTE (PEPPER STRIPS & CORN)

MAKES 4 TO 6 SERVINGS

In a large skillet, melt the butter over medium-low heat. Add the onion and cook, stirring occasionally, until softened, about 5 minutes. Stir in the corn and cook, stirring occasionally, until the corn is just starting to brown, about 5 minutes longer. Add the garlic and cook for 30 seconds more. Add the poblanos, heavy cream, sour cream, cilantro, oregano, and salt. Stir until well combined. Add the Monterey Jack cheese, and cook, stirring occasionally, until melted, 1 to 2 minutes. Stir in the lime juice, then taste and adjust the seasonings, if you like.

Top with the cotija and sprinkle with cilantro. Serve warm as a side dish or with tortillas.

6 serrano chiles, halved lengthwise and seeded

4 ripe plum tomatoes, halved lengthwise

¼ cup water

¼ teaspoon kosher salt

1 tablespoon unsalted butter

½ cup diced yellow onion

10 ounces queso fresco

Tortilla Chips (page 128) or warm flour tortillas, for serving

Nuevo León is a Mexican state along the border. Most of the restaurants there serve chile con queso in the queso fundido style, which is a hot dish dominated by a thick layer of melted cheese. This recipe, however, adapted from one in *La Gran Riqueza de la Cocina Mexicana* by Patricia González, is a salsa-based queso that is more reflective of a dish served at home. Charred chiles and tomatoes make for a robust salsa that goes well with queso fresco. Some brands of queso fresco melt completely while others retain firm curds; both types work in this dish. I like to spoon the queso into flour tortillas but it can be served as a dip, too.

CHILE CON QUESO DE NUEVO LEÓN

MAKES 4 TO 6 SERVINGS

Position a rack 6 inches from the upper heating element and preheat the broiler. Line a baking sheet with aluminum foil.

Place the serranos and tomatoes on the prepared sheet, skin-side up, and broil for 8 to 10 minutes, or until blackened. Place in a blender with the water and salt and blend until smooth.

In a large skillet, melt the butter over medium heat. Add the onion and cook, stirring occasionally, until softened, about 5 minutes. Stir in the serrano-tomato puree, and then crumble in the queso fresco. Cook, stirring, until the cheese has softened, 5 to 7 minutes. Taste and add more salt, if you like.

Transfer the queso to a serving bowl, a small slow cooker, or a chafing dish over a flame. Serve with tortilla chips or warm tortillas.

1 (14.5-ounce) can diced tomatoes, with juices

2 jalapeños, halved lengthwise

2 pequín chiles

4 cloves garlic, peeled

½ cup water

¼ teaspoon kosher salt

½ cup fresh cilantro

1 tablespoon vegetable oil

½ medium yellow onion, thinly sliced

1 pound panela or other non-melting cheese such as paneer or haloumi, cut into ½-inch cubes

Warm flour tortillas, for serving

Some may feel that *queso guisado*, which translates to "stewed cheese," is not a true chile con queso because it's made with a firm cheese that does not melt. But it's still a mixture of chiles (pureed into a piquant tomato salsa) and cheese—although it requires a fork for eating. This dish is commonly found along the border in the Mexican states of Tamaulipas and Nuevo León, though you also see it in Texas in the Rio Grande Valley and in Houston, too. Queso guisado works as a starter as well as a main, especially when matched with refried beans and warm flour tortillas.

▼▲▼▲▼▲▼▲▼▲▼▲▼▲▼▲▼▲▼▲▼▲▼▲

QUESO GUISADO

MAKES 4 TO 6 SERVINGS

In a medium saucepan, combine the tomatoes, jalapeños, pequíns, garlic, water, and salt. Bring to a boil, then turn down the heat to low and simmer, uncovered, for 10 minutes, or until the vegetables have softened. Let cool for 10 minutes.

Pour the tomato mixture into a blender, add the cilantro, and blend until smooth. Measure the salsa; you should have 2 cups. If you're short, add water; if you're a bit over, don't worry about it.

In a large skillet, warm the vegetable oil over medium-low heat. Add the onion and cook, stirring occasionally, until softened, about 5 minutes. Stir in the salsa and add the cheese. Cook for a couple of minutes or until the cheese and salsa are warm. Taste and add more salt, if you like.

To serve, spoon the cheese and sauce onto plates with flour tortillas on the side.

1 tablespoon vegetable oil

½ medium yellow onion, diced

¾ cup diced grape tomatoes

2 cloves garlic, minced

8 Anaheim chiles, roasted (see page 3), peeled, seeded, and chopped

1 cup water

¼ teaspoon kosher salt

4 ounces Chihuahua, asadero, or Muenster cheese, shredded

Tortilla Chips (page 128) and/or warm corn or flour tortillas, for serving

Although the exact origin of chile con queso in Mexico is unknown, today it's most popular in the state of Chihuahua, where it can be served as a side dish, a sauce, or even a dip. Chihuahua's largest city, Juarez, is a sister city to El Paso, and the two have much in common when it comes to cuisine. Chihuahuan chile con queso is much like the queso found in El Paso with its thick blend of roasted chiles and white cheese. The main difference between what one finds in Mexico versus Texas is the emphasis on the chiles, which often dominate the Mexican version of the dish.

CHIHUAHUA CHILE CON QUESO WITH TOMATOES

MAKES 4 SERVINGS

In a medium saucepan, warm the vegetable oil over medium-low heat. Add the onion and cook, stirring occasionally, until softened, about 5 minutes. Add the tomatoes and garlic and cook for 30 seconds longer. Stir in the Anaheims, water, and salt. Cook until warm and fragrant, about 2 minutes. Stir in the cheese and cook until the cheese has melted, about 1 minute. Taste and add more salt, if you like.

Transfer the queso to a serving bowl, a small slow cooker, or a chafing dish over a flame. Serve with tortilla chips and/or warm tortillas.

20 to 25 zucchini squash blossoms

1 tablespoon unsalted butter

¼ cup diced yellow onion

3 cloves garlic, minced

1 poblano chile, roasted (see page 3), peeled, seeded, and finely diced

¼ cup chopped fresh cilantro

½ teaspoon kosher salt

¼ teaspoon ground cumin

1 tablespoon fresh lime juice

1 pound Monterey Jack cheese, shredded

10 warm corn or flour tortillas, for serving

The first time I tried squash blossoms, I was surprised by how savory they were. Instead of being floral and sweet, they tasted more like the zucchini they would have turned into if they hadn't been plucked. One of the more traditional ways to enjoy the blossoms is layered into a quesadilla. This queso fundido pays homage to that dish. You can find squash blossoms at many farmers' markets, some specialty grocers, and in your garden if you grow zucchini. If fresh are unavailable, use canned ones instead.

QUESO FUNDIDO WITH SQUASH BLOSSOMS

MAKES 6 TO 8 SERVINGS

Gently wash the squash blossoms under cold water and remove any bugs that may be hiding. Remove the stems and stamens. Reserve five blossoms for garnish and finely chop the rest.

In a large, broiler-safe skillet, melt the butter over medium-low heat. Add the onion and cook, stirring occasionally, until softened, about 5 minutes. Add the garlic and cook for 30 seconds longer. Stir in the chopped squash blossoms, poblano, cilantro, salt, and cumin and cook, stirring occasionally, until the squash blossoms have softened and released some of their liquid, 2 to 3 minutes. Stir in the lime juice, then taste and adjust the seasonings, if you like. Turn off the heat.

Position a rack 6 inches from the upper heating element and preheat the broiler.

Sprinkle the cheese evenly over the squash blossoms, then arrange the reserved whole squash blossoms on top. Place the skillet under the broiler and cook for 2 minutes, or until the cheese is lightly browned and bubbling. Serve warm with the tortillas.

2 tablespoons unsalted butter

¼ medium yellow onion, thinly sliced

4 cloves garlic, minced

10 ounces cremini mushrooms, sliced

1 or 2 canned chipotle chiles in adobo sauce, finely diced

2 tablespoons chopped fresh cilantro, plus more for garnish

¼ teaspoon dried oregano

¼ teaspoon kosher salt

¼ teaspoon ground cumin

Pinch of cayenne

¼ cup Mexican lager, such as Dos Equis

1 pound Monterey Jack cheese, shredded

1 ounce crumbled cotija or feta cheese

Warm flour tortillas, for serving

Queso flameado means "flamed cheese," a name that derives from cooks pouring alcohol over a dish of shredded cheese and then setting it on fire. The term is interchangeable with *queso fundido,* which means "molten cheese," though the use of one over the other is completely arbitrary, as most places seldom set their queso flameado on fire these days. One of the more popular variations in the Rio Grande Valley is made with mushrooms, which can be as simple as sautéed mushrooms with cheese to more elaborate presentations involving wine and truffles. For mine, I stir in chipotle chiles and a splash of beer for a bit of smoke and tang.

QUESO FLAMEADO WITH MUSHROOMS & CHIPOTLE CHILES

MAKES 6 TO 8 SERVINGS

In a large, ovenproof skillet, melt the butter over medium-low heat. Add the onion and cook, stirring occasionally, until softened, about 5 minutes. Add the garlic and cook for 30 seconds longer. Stir in the mushrooms, chipotles, cilantro, oregano, salt, cumin, cayenne, and lager. Cook, stirring occasionally, until most of the liquid has evaporated, about 5 minutes. Taste and adjust the seasonings, if you like.

Position a rack 6 inches from the upper heating element and preheat the broiler.

Sprinkle the Monterey Jack cheese evenly over the mushrooms. Place the skillet under the broiler and cook for 2 minutes, or until the cheese is lightly browned and bubbling. Garnish with the cotija and cilantro. Serve warm in the skillet with flour tortillas.

MARINATED SHRIMP

1 pound small shrimp, peeled and deveined

2 teaspoons olive oil

2 teaspoons fresh lime juice

¼ teaspoon kosher salt

¼ teaspoon black pepper

Pinch of cayenne

SALSA

½ pound tomatillos, husked

2 jalapeños, halved lengthwise and seeded

⅛ medium yellow onion, peeled

2 cloves garlic, peeled

½ cup fresh cilantro, leaves and stems

½ teaspoon kosher salt

1 tablespoon unsalted butter

1 clove garlic, minced

1 pound Monterey Jack cheese, shredded

Warm tortillas, for serving

In the South Texas town of Kingsville, when I ordered an appetizer called "cheese dip" (rather than chile con queso), I should have known I would be disappointed. Indeed, the waitress set down a bowl filled with a thin yellow concoction that tasted more like a tin can than cheese. When she saw me make a face after I took a bite she said, "Try our Shrimp Queso Flameado instead. It's what we do best." A few minutes later, she brought out a hot dish with thick, oozing layers of white cheese and delicate shrimp, so fresh they were snappy and sweet. I happily ate the whole thing.

▼△▼△▼△▼△▼△▼△▼△▼△▼△▼△▼△▼△

SHRIMP QUESO FLAMEADO WITH JALAPEÑO SALSA

MAKES 6 TO 8 SERVINGS

To marinate the shrimp, in a mixing bowl, toss the shrimp with the olive oil, lime juice, salt, pepper, and cayenne. Set aside.

To make the salsa, in a medium saucepan combine the tomatillos, jalapeños, onion, and garlic. Cover with water and bring to a boil, then turn down the heat to medium-low and simmer, uncovered, for 10 minutes. Let cool for 10 minutes.

With a slotted spoon, transfer the mixture to a blender, leaving behind the liquid. Add the cilantro and salt and blend until smooth. Measure the salsa; you should have 1 cup. If you're short, add water; if you're a bit over, don't worry about it.

In the same pan, melt the butter over medium-low heat and add the garlic and shrimp, along with the marinade. Cook, stirring occasionally, until the shrimp are pink, 2 to 4 minutes. Turn off the heat.

Position a rack 6 inches from the upper heating element and preheat the broiler.

Sprinkle the cheese into a large, broiler-safe skillet. Place the skillet under the broiler and cook for 2 minutes, or until the cheese is lightly browned and bubbling. Pour the salsa over the melted cheese and top with the shrimp.

Serve warm in the skillet with tortillas.

QUIRKY QUESOS

A friend of mine can't eat cheese or milk. He has a genetic disease that prevents him from enjoying a host of foods and, unfortunately, dairy is one of them. There was a time in his life, however, when he didn't restrict his diet, and like most Austinites, a bowl of smooth and creamy queso was a favorite treat.

On a trip home one summer, I offered to cook him and his family dinner. As it was August, which is high season for fresh green chiles, I decided to make tacos with fresh salsa. Of course, no Tex-Mex feast is complete without queso, so I asked if he'd like to be a guinea pig for a new plant-based recipe. He said that would be fantastic.

The next couple of days, as I drove around San Antonio and Austin, any time I came across a vegan queso, I'd give it a try. It was an eye-opening experience. Some strived to taste like regular queso while others didn't try to imitate dairy at all. Some were so good I would eat the whole bowl while others were so awful I'd struggle to swallow one bite. In the end, however, I gained a sense of how to make queso without milk or cheese. And later, when I cooked a batch for my friend, he said it was the best thing he'd had in a long time. He was thrilled to eat queso once again.

I soon discovered that others who abstain from cheese say that queso is the one thing they miss the most. In addition to its velvety comfort, they yearned for the camaraderie found when friends gather around a bowl. Although a nondairy, plant-based queso may seem like an oxymoron, with ingenuity and creativity, one can make a version that's not only a welcome substitute for those who can't eat dairy, but can also be appreciated by those who eat cheese.

Vegan queso isn't the only rendition of the dish that exists outside of the norm. Indeed, chile con queso is flexible and open to many interpretations, and as I drove around Texas, I began to see other quirky adaptations of chiles with cheese. For instance, there's a Mediterranean market in Houston that serves a roux-based queso made with Greek cheeses and spices. In Austin, an Indian bar and restaurant offers a big bowl of melted brick processed cheese garnished with a dollop of spicy jalapeño and cilantro chutney. And friends from East Texas enjoy throwing boudin sausage and crawfish into their queso.

Although these takes on the classic may not fall into either the traditional border or Tex-Mex camps, they are still inviting and fun. But even more important, they show that queso is a dish that is open and accepting to everyone.

1 cup raw unsalted cashews

1 medium carrot, peeled and quartered

1 cup unsweetened almond milk

2 cups water

¼ cup nutritional yeast

2 tablespoons cornstarch

1 tablespoon vegetable oil

¼ cup diced yellow onion

2 jalapeños, seeded and diced

2 cloves garlic, minced

1 (10-ounce) can diced tomatoes with green chiles, with juices

1 teaspoon kosher salt

1 teaspoon ground cumin

1 teaspoon garlic powder

½ teaspoon celery salt

¼ teaspoon cayenne

2 tablespoons fresh lime juice

½ cup chopped fresh cilantro

Pico de gallo (page 125), for topping

Tortilla Chips (page 128), for serving

Austin has a long-standing reputation as the hippie capital of Texas, so it's no surprise that nondairy, plant-based quesos are popular there. The version I enjoyed in San Antonio (see page 82) was made with vegan cheese, but most of the ones I sampled in Austin used a nut-and-vegetable base. The latter will appeal to those who may prefer a less-processed dish. A smooth blend of cashews mixed with a bit of carrot for color provides a creamy foundation, then a host of spices along with canned chiles give this dip that familiar tang and flavor.

▽△▽△▽△▽△▽△▽△▽△▽△▽△▽△▽△▽△

AUSTIN-STYLE VEGAN QUESO

MAKES 4 TO 6 SERVINGS

Cover the cashews with water and let soak for 1 hour. Meanwhile, in a small saucepan, cover the carrot with water, bring to a boil, and cook until tender, 5 to 7 minutes. Drain and transfer to a blender. Drain the cashews and add to the blender with the almond milk, water, nutritional yeast, and cornstarch. Blend until smooth.

In a medium saucepan, warm the vegetable oil over medium-low heat. Add the onion and jalapeños and cook, stirring occasionally, until softened, about 5 minutes. Add the garlic and cook for 30 seconds longer. Pour the carrot-cashew puree into the pan and cook, stirring, for a couple of minutes, until the mixture begins to thicken. Stir in the tomatoes, salt, cumin, garlic powder, celery salt, cayenne, lime juice, and cilantro. Taste and adjust the seasonings, if you like.

Transfer the queso to a serving bowl, a small slow cooker, or a chafing dish over a flame and spoon pico de gallo on top. Serve warm with tortilla chips.

NOTE: Guacamole, bean dip, black beans, and vegan sausage are also good with this queso.

1 tablespoon vegetable oil

¼ cup diced yellow onion

2 jalapeños, seeded and diced

2 cloves garlic, minced

2 tablespoons cornstarch

2 cups unsweetened almond milk

14 ounces to 1 pound shredded vegan cheese (see Note)

1 (10-ounce) can diced tomatoes with green chiles, with juices

½ teaspoon ground cumin

¼ teaspoon granulated garlic

¼ teaspoon celery salt

Pinch of cayenne

¼ cup chopped fresh cilantro

1 tablespoon fresh lime juice

Kosher salt

Pico de Gallo (page 125), for topping

Tortilla Chips (page 128), for serving

San Antonio Tex-Mex cuisine skews more traditional, but a restaurant there called Viva Vegaria specializes in vegan Tex-Mex. Out of curiosity, I ordered the queso and I was shocked at how much I loved it. The waiter told me that it had a base of almond milk and vegan cheese, and that the addition of canned tomatoes with green chiles is what gave it that authentic flavor. I've done the same with my recipe, and if you close your eyes as you have a taste, you might not even realize it's a plant-based queso.

SAN ANTONIO-STYLE VEGAN QUESO

MAKES 4 TO 6 SERVINGS

In a medium saucepan, warm the vegetable oil over medium-low heat. Add the onion and jalapeños and cook, stirring occasionally, until softened, about 5 minutes. Add the garlic and cook for 30 seconds longer.

Whisk together the cornstarch and almond milk until well combined and then pour into the pan, along with the cheese. Bring to a simmer, stirring constantly, then turn down the heat to low and cook, stirring, until the cheese has melted. Stir in the tomatoes, cumin, granulated garlic, celery salt, cayenne, cilantro, and lime juice. Taste and adjust the seasonings, adding salt, if you like.

Transfer the queso to a serving bowl, a small slow cooker, or a chafing dish over a flame and top with pico de gallo. Serve warm with tortilla chips.

NOTE: My favorite cheese for this recipe is American cheese made by Follow Your Heart, which comes in 7-ounce packages. Daiya's Cheddar and pepper Jack shreds are in 8-ounce packages; a mixture of the two Daiya cheeses is also tasty.

CHUTNEY

2 jalapeños, seeded and chopped

2 cloves garlic

½ cup fresh cilantro

2 tablespoons olive oil

2 tablespoons fresh lime juice

1 tablespoon unsweetened flaked coconut

½ teaspoon ground cumin

¼ teaspoon kosher salt

Pinch of ground ginger

QUESO

1 pound brick processed cheese, cubed

½ cup whole milk

½ teaspoon ground cumin

½ teaspoon paprika

¼ teaspoon cayenne

Cilantro leaves, for garnish

Tortilla Chips (page 128), for serving

Texas has a strong Asian Indian community, and since Tex-Mex and Indian cuisines both embrace chiles, cilantro, and spices such as cumin, dishes that unite the two are becoming more common. One example of this fusion is Indian-style queso. The version I've included here is similar to one served at Austin's Whip In, a lively Indian restaurant and bar. Its foundation is traditional, as it's made with melted brick processed cheese. What makes this queso truly stand apart from others is the chutney topping made with jalapeños, cilantro, coconut, and ginger. This dip is both familiar and fresh, and a fine example of how Texan queso culture is evolving.

INDIAN QUESO WITH JALAPEÑO CHUTNEY

MAKES 4 TO 6 SERVINGS

To make the chutney, place the jalapeños, garlic, cilantro, olive oil, lime juice, coconut, cumin, salt, and ginger in a food processor or blender. Puree until smooth. Taste and adjust the seasonings, if you like.

To make the queso, in a medium saucepan, combine the cheese, milk, cumin, paprika, and cayenne. Cook over low heat, stirring, until the cheese has melted. Taste and adjust the seasonings, if you like.

Transfer the queso to a serving bowl, a small slow cooker, or a chafing dish over a flame. Top with the chutney and garnish with cilantro leaves. Serve warm with tortilla chips.

½ teaspoon dried oregano

½ teaspoon kosher salt

½ teaspoon black pepper

¼ teaspoon ground cinnamon

¼ teaspoon cayenne

¾ cup diced grape tomatoes

2 ounces feta cheese

½ cup diced pitted kalamata olives

2 tablespoons diced red onion

4 jalapeños, seeded and diced

2 cloves garlic, minced

1 tablespoon olive oil

1 tablespoon fresh lemon juice

2 tablespoons chopped flat-leaf parsley

2 tablespoons unsalted butter

2 tablespoons all-purpose flour

1½ cups whole milk

8 ounces white Cheddar cheese, shredded

4 ounces Gouda cheese, shredded

4 ounces Kefalograviera or Gruyère cheese, shredded

½ cup sour cream

Pita chips, for serving

Houston's MKT Bar serves a dish called Greek Queso made with Kefalograviera, a Greek sheep's-milk cheese similar to Gruyère, and Beemster, a semisoft Dutch cheese much like Gouda. For my take, I've added a Mediterranean inspired salsa made with olives, feta, and jalapeños. If you can't find Kefalograviera, the queso is still excellent with its more readily available substitution.

GREEK QUESO

MAKES 6 TO 8 SERVINGS

In a small bowl, whisk together the oregano, salt, pepper, cinnamon, and cayenne. In a medium bowl, stir together the tomatoes, feta, olives, red onion, half the jalapeños, half the garlic, the olive oil, lemon juice, parsley, and half the oregano mixture. Taste and adjust the seasonings, if you like, and set aside.

In a medium saucepan, melt the butter over medium-low heat. Add the remaining jalapeños and cook, stirring occasionally, until softened, about 5 minutes. Add the remaining garlic and cook for 30 seconds longer. Whisk in the flour, bring to a simmer, and cook until lightly browned and nutty, about 1 minute. Add the milk and cook, stirring occasionally, until just beginning to thicken, about 2 minutes.

Turn down the heat to low and stir in the Cheddar, Beemster, and Kefalograviera cheeses, one handful at a time. After each handful has melted into the sauce, repeat with the next. Stir in the remaining oregano mixture and the sour cream until well combined, then taste and adjust the seasonings, if you like.

Transfer the queso to a serving bowl, a small slow cooker, or a chafing dish over a flame and top with the tomato-feta mixture. Serve warm with pita chips.

3 jalapeños, halved and seeded

¼ red onion

1 clove garlic

¼ cup cilantro leaves

2 tablespoons white vinegar

½ teaspoon kosher salt

¼ teaspoon ground cumin

1 (16-ounce) container small-curd creamed (4%) cottage cheese

1 avocado, halved, pitted, peeled, and diced

Tortilla Chips (page 128), for serving

Crudités, for serving

This recipe, adapted from one found in El Paso's Junior League cookbook *Seasoned with Sun,* has a cottage cheese base. The dish might sound strange, but it's actually very refreshing. The original called for a jarred pepper relish, but I prefer the brighter, crisper flavors that come from whirring fresh jalapeños with aromatics and vinegar. The resulting relish, combined with the cottage cheese and diced avocado, is welcome on hot days. And it's easy on your waistline!

CHILLED CHILE CON QUESO WITH AVOCADO

MAKES 6 TO 8 SERVINGS

Put the jalapeños, onion, garlic, cilantro, vinegar, salt, and cumin in a food processor and pulse until finely minced.

Combine the jalapeño mixture with the cottage cheese and avocado. Taste and adjust the seasonings, if you like.

Serve immediately with tortilla chips and crudités.

2 tablespoons unsalted butter

¼ cup diced yellow onion

½ red bell pepper, seeded and diced

2 jalapeños, seeded and diced

2 cloves garlic, minced

1 cup lager, such as Lone Star or Corona

1 cup water

8 ounces cream cheese, at room temperature

1 pound white American cheese, shredded

1 pound lump crabmeat

2 tablespoons chopped fresh cilantro

1 tablespoon fresh lime juice, plus 1 teaspoon grated lime zest

½ teaspoon kosher salt

¼ teaspoon cayenne

Guacamole (page 125), for topping

Tortilla Chips (page 128), for serving

In the late summer and early fall, crabs are in season along the Texas Gulf Coast. During this time, crab boils are popular, and people will gather at tables with wooden mallets, dipping sauces, and a bucket of cold beverages to enjoy the bounty. This queso pays homage to those milder days, when the most pressing concern is how much you can eat before you get full.

GULF COAST CRAB QUESO

MAKES 6 TO 8 SERVINGS

In a medium saucepan, melt the butter over medium-low heat. Add the onion, bell pepper, and jalapeños and cook, stirring occasionally, until softened, about 5 minutes. Add the garlic and cook for 30 seconds longer. Add the lager, water, cream cheese, and American cheese. Turn down the heat to low and cook, stirring, until the cheese has melted. Reserve ¼ cup of crabmeat for garnish and stir in the remaining crab with the cilantro, lime juice, salt, and cayenne. Cook until the crabmeat is warm, a couple of minutes. Taste and adjust the seasonings, if you like.

Transfer the queso to a serving bowl, a small slow cooker, or a chafing dish over a flame. Sprinkle with the lime zest, spoon guacamole onto the center of the queso, and top with the reserved crab. Serve warm with tortilla chips.

1 tablespoon
unsalted butter

¼ cup diced yellow onion

2 cloves garlic, minced

½ cup fresh or thawed
frozen corn kernels

2 canned chipotle chiles
in adobo sauce, diced

2 tablespoons
cornstarch

1 cup whole milk

1 cup water

1 pound white American
cheese, shredded

12 ounces frozen shelled
crawfish tails, thawed

1 teaspoon kosher salt

1 teaspoon ground
cumin

¼ teaspoon smoked
paprika

¼ teaspoon celery salt

2 tablespoons fresh
lime juice

2 tablespoons chopped
fresh cilantro, plus more
for garnish

Tortilla Chips (page 128),
for serving

Crawfish is in season in the spring and it's abundant throughout Texas and Louisiana during this time. The most common way to enjoy the crustaceans is to boil them whole; people also take the meat from the tail and include it in a host of dishes—from Cajun standards, such as étouffée, to more creative applications, such as chile con queso. Here, I've added corn, which is a classic pairing with the sweet meat, and smoky chipotle chiles as a nod to the crawfish often being boiled over flames outdoors. Frozen crawfish tails are available year-round and work well when fresh isn't available.

▼△▼△▼△▼△▼△▼△▼△▼△▼△▼△▼△▼△▼△

EAST TEXAS CRAWFISH QUESO

MAKES 6 TO 8 SERVINGS

In a medium saucepan, melt the butter over medium-low heat. Add the onion and cook, stirring occasionally, until softened, about 5 minutes. Add the garlic, corn, and chipotles, and cook for 30 seconds longer.

Whisk together the cornstarch, milk, and water until well combined, then pour into the pan. Bring to a simmer, stirring constantly, and cook for a couple of minutes, until the mixture begins to thicken. Add the cheese and cook, stirring, until melted.

Season the crawfish tails with the salt, cumin, smoked paprika, celery salt, and lime juice and stir into the queso with the cilantro. Cook until the tails are warmed through, a couple of minutes. Taste and adjust the seasonings, if you like.

Transfer the queso to a serving bowl, a small slow cooker, or a chafing dish over a flame. Garnish with more cilantro and serve warm with tortilla chips.

1 tablespoon bacon grease

4 ounces ground pork

4 ounces chicken livers, finely chopped

½ teaspoon kosher salt

¼ medium yellow onion, finely diced

1 celery rib, finely diced

4 jalapeños, seeded and finely diced

2 cloves garlic, minced

1 cup cooked long-grain white rice

½ teaspoon dried thyme

½ teaspoon dried oregano

½ teaspoon smoked paprika

¼ teaspoon celery salt

¼ teaspoon cayenne

4 green onions, chopped, green parts only

¼ cup chopped fresh flat-leaf parsley

½ cup water

1 pound brick processed cheese, cubed

2 tablespoons whole milk

1 (10-ounce) can diced tomatoes with green chiles, with juices

Louisiana-style hot sauce, for drizzling

Tortilla Chips (page 128), for serving

Boudin is a Cajun sausage made with rice, pork, and either chicken or pork liver. It's a stuffed sausage, but most folks squeeze the filling out of the casing before eating it with a stack of crackers, a dash of hot sauce, and a cold beverage or two. I know people who will add boudin to just about anything—eggs, gumbo, and, yes, even queso. Unfortunately, it's difficult to find outside of Louisiana and Texas. But this recipe offers the inner workings of boudin, which is then added to a blend of melted cheese and canned tomatoes with green chiles.

▼△▼△▼△▼△▼△▼△▼△▼△▼△▼△▼△▼△▼△

BOUDIN QUESO

MAKES 6 TO 8 SERVINGS

In a large skillet, warm the bacon grease over medium-low heat. Add the pork, chicken livers, and salt and cook, stirring occasionally, until brown and crisp, about 5 minutes. Add the onion, celery, and jalapeños and continue to cook, stirring occasionally, until the vegetables are softened, about 5 minutes. Add the garlic and cook for 30 seconds longer. Add the rice, thyme, oregano, smoked paprika, celery salt, cayenne, half the green onions, half the parsley, and the water. Stir until well combined. Continue to cook, stirring occasionally, until most of the liquid has evaporated, about 5 minutes. Taste and adjust the seasonings, if you like, and then turn off the heat.

In a medium saucepan, combine the cheese, milk, and tomatoes. Cook over low heat, stirring occasionally, until the cheese has melted.

Transfer the queso to a serving bowl, a small slow cooker, or a chafing dish over a flame. Stir in the rice mixture and garnish with the remaining green onions, remaining parsley, and a generous drizzle of hot sauce. Serve warm with tortilla chips.

2 tablespoons
unsalted butter

8 ounces smoked
sausage, such as
kielbasa, diced

¼ cup diced yellow
onion

4 jalapeños, seeded
and diced

2 tablespoons
cornstarch

1 cup water

1 cup Texas dark beer,
such as Shiner Bock

8 ounces smoked
Cheddar cheese,
shredded

8 ounces yellow
American cheese,
shredded

½ teaspoon powdered
mustard

¼ teaspoon dried dill

¼ teaspoon cayenne

¼ teaspoon kosher salt

Pickled Jalapeños
(page 126), for garnish

Tortilla Chips (page 128)
and/or soft pretzels, for
serving

In the 1800s, German immigrants settled in the Hill Country region of Central Texas, and their influence is still strongly reflected in the local cuisine. German favorites such as spicy sausage, dark beer, tangy mustard, and a pinch of dill all lend flavor to this Central Texas–inspired queso. A handful of jalapeños and a dash of cayenne give it some heat.

▼△▼△▼△▼△▼△▼△▼△▼△▼△▼

HILL COUNTRY SAUSAGE QUESO

MAKES 6 TO 8 SERVINGS

In a medium saucepan, melt the butter over medium-low heat. Add the sausage and cook, stirring occasionally, until beginning to brown and some of the fat has rendered, about 5 minutes. Add the onion and jalapeños and cook, stirring occasionally, until softened, about 5 minutes longer.

Whisk together the cornstarch, water, and beer until well combined, then pour into the pan. Bring to a simmer, stirring constantly, and cook until the mixture begins to thicken. Add both cheeses, turn down the heat to low, and cook, stirring, until the cheeses have melted. Stir in the mustard, dill, cayenne, and salt, then taste and adjust the seasonings, if you like.

Transfer the queso to a serving bowl, a small slow cooker, or a chafing dish over a flame. Garnish with pickled jalapeños. Serve warm with tortilla chips and/or soft pretzels.

SCIENTIFIC QUESO

Processed cheeses, namely American cheese and Velveeta, are key to producing a classic bowl of Tex-Mex chile con queso, but due to availability and/or personal preferences, some people like to make their dip with a non-processed cheese such as Cheddar, pepper Jack, or Gruyère. Non-processed cheese requires a starch, usually either flour or cornstarch, to prevent the cheese from turning into a clumpy, greasy mess when it's melted into the queso base, and although this method works quite well, some folks feel the starch detracts from the taste of the cheese.

A few years ago, however, a reader told me she had learned a new way to make a chile con queso with real cheese that didn't call for starch yet still achieved the velvety mouthfeel of processed cheese. It was a game changer, she said, and she could now make queso with her favorite sharp Cheddar, and it would be as smooth and silky as one made with Velveeta. The secret? Sodium citrate, which she had read about in *Modernist Cuisine at Home*, a molecular gastronomy cookbook by Nathan Myhrvold and Maxime Bilet. The authors explain that sodium citrate, a salt, helps the fat and water emulsion in dairy products stay together when heat is applied, so even non-processed cheese melts into a creamy sauce. The use of sodium citrate has become popular with makers of classic French cheese sauces, and even with queso cooks who prefer real cheese in their dip.

Recipes using sodium citrate usually list the ingredients by weight, but many home-kitchen scales are not precise enough to weigh the minute amount of sodium citrate needed. So here is a recipe by volume. For the liquid, don't use anything containing salt because the sodium citrate is salty enough. You can add chiles, aromatics, spices, vegetables, meats, or any other flavorings to the finished sauce to turn it into chile con queso. The possibilities are endless and only limited by your imagination! Sodium citrate can be purchased at many spice shops and online at kalustyans.com.

Sodium Citrate Cheese Sauce
Makes 4 servings

1 teaspoon sodium citrate
½ cup liquid, such as water or beer
2 cups (8 ounces) shredded non-processed cheese, such as Cheddar or Monterey Jack

Stir together the sodium citrate and liquid in a medium saucepan and cook over medium-low heat until warm. Add the cheese and cook, stirring constantly, until melted and smooth.

QUESO IN THE WILD

The H&H Car Wash and Coffee Shop in El Paso is a bustling spot for breakfast and lunch. Several ladies stand behind a turquoise counter taking orders with brisk efficiency, while the cook deftly prepares eggs and burritos on a sizzling griddle. The morning I visited, the restaurant was packed with chatty customers who all seemed to know one another.

Soon after I took my seat, a large man came in from the car wash and greeted everyone with back pats, handshakes, and a smile. He made his way to me, and said, "Hello and welcome!" I returned the greeting and he introduced himself as the owner, Maynard Haddad, and asked if I was new to the area. I laughed and asked if it was obvious I wasn't from El Paso. He explained that H&H was the sort of place that's filled with regulars and when someone new arrives, he wants to make their acquaintance.

So I told him that I was visiting the area for a few days, and then the people sitting next to me joined in on the conversation. We began to talk and before long, I had a new group of friends. H&H was easily one of the friendliest places I'd visited on my travels.

As we were chatting, the waitress slid a plate in front of the woman next to me. It appeared to be two fried eggs sitting on a crisp tostada smothered in a creamy yellow sauce, which looked suspiciously like queso. In El Paso, the queso is typically made with white, non-processed cheese, but this was processed cheese queso, that sunny elixir you find far from the border.

he woman saw me staring at her plate and said, "These are huevos rancheros." Haddad chimed in that the dish was his number-one seller. A man sitting to my right said they were also his favorite. Then I looked around the room and saw several others tucking into these eggs smothered in melted cheese. Although I had been satisfied with my carne picada, flour tortillas, and refried beans, I realized that maybe I should have ordered the huevos rancheros.

Perhaps seeing the longing on my face, the woman offered me a bite from her plate, but feeling shy, I declined, saying I would order it some other time. I was struck by her kindness and generosity, which confirmed for me that whenever queso is present, good things happen and connections are made.

Now, here's the thing, huevos rancheros are usually topped with a tomato salsa, so the yellow queso in El Paso is unusual. I later surmised it was perhaps a nod to ranchero cheese, a popular cheese made by ranchers across the border in the Mexican state of Chihuahua, but this doesn't explain why in El Paso they use processed cheese instead. Unfortunately, no one had any answers or knew the dish's origin, but it didn't matter— I had discovered queso in the wild.

Since then, there have been other unlikely queso appearances. There was the chicken-fried steak smothered in queso in San Antonio; the 1970s salad recipe calling for queso dressing; the cocktail-party sausage balls made with cheese and a certain canned tomato with chiles that gave it a distinctly queso-like essence. I even had a green chile ice cream sundae in New Mexico that locals told me was their favorite chile con queso of all. What a joy to discover queso in myriad new and delicious forms!

1 tablespoon unsalted butter

2 tablespoons diced yellow onion

1 jalapeño, seeded and diced

2 cloves garlic, minced

¾ cup diced grape tomatoes

1 tablespoon cornstarch

¾ cup whole milk

½ cup water

8 ounces yellow American cheese, shredded

½ teaspoon kosher salt

½ teaspoon ground cumin

¼ teaspoon cayenne

8 Crispy Tostadas (see variation, page 128)

2 teaspoons vegetable oil

8 large eggs

Chopped fresh cilantro, for garnish

Hot sauce, for serving (optional)

In El Paso, huevos rancheros, which translates to "ranch eggs," are topped with queso instead of the more common tomato-based sauce, something I initially found odd. But once I learned that Mexican ranchers right across the border are renowned for making cheese, the name made more sense. Even more curious is that the sauce is made with yellow American cheese instead of white cheeses, such as the Muenster or Monterey Jack traditionally used in El Paso–style queso (see page 62). No matter, the dish is a fine way to begin the day.

EL PASO-STYLE HUEVOS RANCHEROS

MAKES 4 SERVINGS

In a medium saucepan, melt the butter over medium-low heat. Add the onion and jalapeño and cook, stirring occasionally, until softened, about 5 minutes. Add the garlic and tomatoes and cook for 30 seconds longer.

Whisk together the cornstarch, milk, and water until well combined, then pour into the pan. Bring to a simmer, stirring constantly, and cook for a couple of minutes, until thickened. Add the cheese, turn down the heat to low, and cook, stirring, until the cheese has melted. Stir in the salt, cumin, and cayenne, then taste and adjust the seasonings, if you like. Keep the queso over low heat, stirring occasionally to prevent burning.

CONTINUED

Place two tostadas on each of four plates.

In a large skillet, warm 1 teaspoon of the vegetable oil over medium heat. One at time, crack 4 eggs into the skillet, lightly salt them, and fry until the whites and yolks are set to your preference, about 2 minutes for over easy, 3 minutes for over hard. Place a cooked egg on each tostada. Repeat with the remaining oil and eggs.

Stir the queso and evenly drizzle over the eggs. Garnish with cilantro and serve immediately with hot sauce, if desired.

1 (15-ounce) can black beans, drained and rinsed

1 cup diced grape tomatoes

4 jalapeños, seeded and diced

¼ cup diced red onion

2 cloves garlic, minced

¼ cup chopped fresh cilantro

2 tablespoons fresh lime juice

1 teaspoon olive oil

1 teaspoon kosher salt

1 teaspoon ground cumin

¼ teaspoon cayenne

1 tablespoon unsalted butter

1 tablespoon cornstarch

½ cup whole milk

½ cup water

8 ounces yellow American cheese, shredded

1 head iceberg lettuce, outer leaves discarded, quartered

2 cups Fritos corn chips

Frito salad made with iceburg lettuce, tomatoes, beans, and said corn chips has long been a dinnertime mainstay in Texan homes. Typically it's dressed with vinaigrette, but in 1972, an article in the *Naples Monitor* suggested using queso instead. Trying this idea as a tossed salad, I found that the cheese got lost in the tangle. But if you drizzle the sunny dressing over an iceberg wedge before showering it with toppings, the queso really shines.

▽△▽△▽△▽△▽△▽△▽△▽△▽△▽△▽△

FRITO WEDGE SALAD WITH QUESO DRESSING

MAKES 4 SERVINGS

Stir together the black beans, tomatoes, half the jalapeños, half the onion, half the garlic, the cilantro, lime juice, and olive oil. Combine the salt, cumin, and cayenne, then stir half this spice mixture into the black bean mixture. Taste and adjust the seasonings, if you like.

In a medium saucepan, melt the butter over medium-low heat. Add the remaining jalapeños and remaining onion and cook, stirring occasionally, until softened, about 5 minutes. Add the remaining garlic and cook for 30 seconds longer.

Whisk together the cornstarch, milk, and water until well combined, then pour into the pan. Bring to a simmer, stirring constantly, and cook for a couple of minutes, until the mixture begins to thicken. Add the cheese, turn down the heat to low, and cook, stirring, until the cheese has melted. Stir in the remaining spice mixture, then taste and adjust the seasonings, if you like.

Place an iceberg wedge on each of four plates. Pour the queso dressing over the wedges, dividing it evenly, and top with the black beans and Fritos. Serve immediately.

1 pound ground pork

1 tablespoon brown sugar

1 tablespoon dried rubbed sage

1 teaspoon dried thyme

1 teaspoon kosher salt

1 teaspoon black pepper

½ teaspoon ground cumin

½ teaspoon red pepper flakes

¼ teaspoon cayenne

1½ cups all-purpose flour

½ cup yellow cornmeal

2 teaspoons baking powder

8 ounces Cheddar cheese, shredded

1 (10-ounce) can diced tomatoes with green chiles, with juices

In Texas, during the holidays, sausage balls are a beloved nibble. For those not familiar with them, sausage balls—made of loose sausage, flour, and cheese—are a biscuit-meatball hybrid. Versions calling for canned tomatoes with green chiles and yellow Cheddar cheese are usually called chile con queso sausage balls. Although spicy chorizo may seem a more obvious choice for the meat, my preference is breakfast sausage. These are not a fancy snack but will definitely be a popular one. You may want to double the recipe since they always go fast.

▼△▼△▼△▼△▼△▼△▼△▼△▼△▼△▼△▼△▼

CHILE CON QUESO SAUSAGE BALLS

MAKES 8 TO 10 SERVINGS (ABOUT 48 BALLS)

Preheat the oven to 350°F and line two baking sheets with parchment paper or grease them with cooking spray.

In a mixing bowl, combine the pork, brown sugar, sage, thyme, salt, pepper, cumin, red pepper flakes, and cayenne. Add the flour, cornmeal, baking powder, cheese, and tomatoes and, using your hands or a spoon, mix until well combined.

Scoop out 1 tablespoonful of the dough and roll it into a ball. Place the balls ½ inch apart on the prepared baking sheets. Bake for 25 to 30 minutes, rotating the sheets after 15 minutes, until the sausage is cooked, the cheese has melted, and the tops of the balls are lightly browned. Serve warm.

1 cup whole milk

1 cup water

2 tablespoons cornstarch

1 pound yellow American cheese, shredded

2 teaspoons chili powder

2 teaspoons ground cumin

½ teaspoon paprika

½ teaspoon granulated garlic

½ teaspoon powdered mustard

¼ teaspoon kosher salt

1 tablespoon vegetable oil

2 cups chili without beans (see page 44)

4 beef or pork tamales (about 5 ounces each), unwrapped and cut into ½-inch pieces

2 cups crushed Fritos or other corn chips

¼ cup diced yellow onion

2 jalapeños, sliced into rounds

Saltines or Tortilla Chips (page 128), for serving

This is what happens when tamale pie meets Frito pie. And because that's not decadent enough, I smother it with queso. This was originally inspired by a dip served at Little Rock's Heights Taco & Tamale Co., but I feel it works better served in bowls and eaten with a spoon. To balance all the meat and cheese, the traditional chili garnishes of sliced jalapeños and diced onion are a must.

TAMALE CHILI PIE

MAKES 6 TO 8 SERVINGS

In a medium saucepan, whisk together the milk, water, and cornstarch. Bring to a simmer over medium-low heat, stirring constantly, and cook for a couple minutes until the mixture begins to thicken. Add the cheese and turn down the heat to low. Cook, stirring, until the cheese has melted. Stir in the chili powder, cumin, paprika, granulated garlic, mustard, and salt. Taste and adjust the seasonings, if you like. Cover the pan and turn down the heat to low to keep the queso warm as you finish the dish.

In a large skillet, warm the vegetable oil over medium-low heat. Add the chili and tamales and cook, stirring, until warmed through, about 5 minutes. Stir in the Fritos. Top with the queso and sprinkle evenly with the onion and jalapeños.

Serve warm in bowls with saltines or tortilla chips.

2 cups elbow macaroni

1 tablespoon unsalted butter

¼ cup diced yellow onion

2 cloves garlic, minced

8 Anaheim chiles, roasted (see page 3), peeled, seeded, and finely diced

1½ cups heavy cream

8 ounces Monterey Jack cheese, shredded

8 ounces white Cheddar cheese, shredded

½ teaspoon kosher salt

½ teaspoon ground cumin

¼ teaspoon cayenne

1 cup finely crushed Tortilla Chips (page 128)

Chopped fresh cilantro, for garnish

Usually when chile con queso macaroni and cheese is offered, it's prepared with yellow processed cheese. Don't get me wrong— it's tasty stuff, but I prefer different cheeses with my pasta. Inspired by the quesos found in West Texas, I took the basic dish and used Monterey Jack and white Cheddar instead. I also dialed up the amount of green chiles and, to finish, added crushed tortilla chips on top. This recipe takes little effort but yields a big reward.

MACARONI & CHEESE WITH GREEN CHILE QUESO BLANCO

MAKES 8 SERVINGS

Bring a large pot of salted water to a boil and add the macaroni. Cook according to the package directions, then drain the pasta.

In a large, broiler-safe skillet, melt the butter over medium-low heat. Add the onion and cook, stirring occasionally, until softened, about 5 minutes. Add the garlic and Anaheims and cook for 30 seconds longer. Add the pasta, cream, half the Monterey Jack, and half the Cheddar. Cook, stirring, until the cheeses have melted, about 2 minutes. Stir in the salt, cumin, and cayenne, then taste and adjust the seasonings, if you like.

Position a rack 6 inches from the upper heating element and preheat the broiler.

Evenly top the macaroni with the remaining Monterey Jack and Cheddar, then sprinkle with the crushed tortilla chips. Place the skillet under the broiler and cook for 1 to 2 minutes, or until the cheese is lightly browned and bubbling. Garnish with cilantro and serve warm.

2 tablespoons unsalted butter

¼ cup diced yellow onion

4 jalapeños, seeded and diced

2 cloves garlic, minced

2 tablespoons cornstarch

1 cup whole milk

1 cup water

1 pound yellow American cheese, shredded

¾ cup diced grape tomatoes

½ teaspoon kosher salt

½ teaspoon ground cumin

¼ teaspoon cayenne

2 tablespoons vegetable oil

12 corn tortillas

12 ounces Colby Jack cheese, shredded

The soft cheese taco is a Dallas-area specialty that is less a taco and more a cheese enchilada smothered in chile con queso instead of the chili gravy typical of Tex-Mex enchiladas. Besides the odd name, what also makes the dish unusual is that the cheese in the filling is often Cheddar or Monterey Jack but the queso drizzled on top is always made with American cheese.

▽△▽△▽△▽△▽△▽△▽△▽△▽△▽△▽

SOFT CHEESE TACOS

MAKES 4 TO 6 SERVINGS

Preheat the oven to 350°F.

In a medium saucepan, melt the butter over medium-low heat. Add the onion and jalapeños and cook, stirring occasionally, until softened, about 5 minutes. Add the garlic and cook for 30 seconds longer.

Whisk together the cornstarch, milk, and water until well combined, then pour into the pan. Bring to a simmer, stirring constantly, and cook for a couple of minutes, until the mixture begins to thicken. Add the American cheese, turn down the heat to low, and cook, stirring, until the cheese has melted. Add the tomatoes and stir to combine. Stir in the salt, cumin, and cayenne, then taste and adjust the seasonings, if you like. Turn off the heat.

Pour the vegetable oil into a 9 by 13-inch baking dish. Place the tortillas in the baking dish (it's okay if they overlap) and turn each one to coat with oil. Place uncovered in the oven for 3 to 5 minutes, or until the tortillas are soft and warm. Remove the tortillas from the baking dish and keep covered.

Place a warm tortilla on a clean surface, add ¼ cup of the Colby Jack down the center of the tortilla, and roll up the tortilla. Arrange the rolled taco seam-side down in the baking dish. Repeat with the remaining tortillas and Colby Jack. Cover the baking dish with aluminum foil and bake until the cheese in the tortillas has melted, 10 to 15 minutes. Meanwhile, reheat the queso over low heat, stirring occasionally. Remove the tacos from the oven, uncover, and pour the queso evenly over the top. Serve warm.

CHILI-CHEESE ENCHILADAS

After the cheese in the tortillas has melted, top with 2 cups hot chili (see page 44) before pouring on the queso.

½ pound tomatillos, husked

4 cloves garlic

4 jalapeños, halved and seeded

1 cup fresh cilantro, plus chopped cilantro for garnish

¼ teaspoon ground cumin

1 cup water

½ teaspoon kosher salt

2 Anaheim chiles, roasted (see page 3), peeled, seeded, and diced

1 pound brick processed cheese, cubed

2 tablespoons vegetable oil

12 corn tortillas

2 cups shredded cooked chicken

8 ounces Monterey Jack cheese, shredded

¼ cup diced red onion

Here we have corn tortillas stuffed with chicken and Monterey Jack. They are baked with salsa verde, and smothered with green chile queso. I call them enchiladas, which may seem obvious yet it took a while to come up with this designation. See, in Texas, rolled tortillas stuffed with cheese and topped with queso are known as "soft cheese tacos," but if one stuffs the tortillas with meat before smothering it with queso, they're called enchiladas. It's a nomenclatural mystery I haven't been able to solve. But to paraphrase Shakespeare, a soft taco by any other name tastes just as sweet.

CHICKEN ENCHILADAS WITH GREEN CHILE QUESO

MAKES 4 TO 6 SERVINGS

Preheat the oven to 350°F.

Place the tomatillos, garlic, jalapeños, cilantro, cumin, water, and salt in a blender and blend until smooth.

In a medium saucepan, combine ½ cup of the tomatillo mixture, half the Anaheims, and the processed cheese. Cook over medium-low heat, stirring, until the cheese has melted. Taste and adjust the seasonings, adding salt if you like. Turn off the heat.

CONTINUED

Pour the vegetable oil into a 9 by 13-inch baking dish. Place the tortillas in the baking dish (it's okay if they overlap) and turn each one to coat with oil. Place uncovered in the oven for 3 to 5 minutes, or until the tortillas are soft and warm. Remove the tortillas from the baking dish and keep covered. Pour half of the remaining tomatillo mixture into the baking dish.

Stir together the chicken, Monterey Jack, remaining Anaheims, and half the onion. Taste the filling, adding salt, if you like.

Place a warm tortilla on a clean surface, add ¼ cup filling down the center of the tortilla, then roll up the tortilla. Arrange the rolled tortilla seam-side down in the baking dish. Repeat with the remaining tortillas and filling. Top with the remaining tomatillo mixture, cover the baking dish with aluminum foil, and bake until the cheese in the tortillas has melted, 10 to 15 minutes.

Meanwhile, reheat the queso over low heat, stirring occasionally.

Remove the enchiladas from the oven, uncover, and pour the queso evenly over the top. Garnish with cilantro and the remaining onion. Serve warm.

QUESO

1 tablespoon unsalted butter

¼ cup diced yellow onion

2 tablespoons cornstarch

1 cup whole milk

1 cup water

1 pound yellow American cheese, shredded

½ teaspoon ground cumin

¼ teaspoon kosher salt

¼ teaspoon cayenne

¼ cup diced Pickled Jalapeños (page 126)

2 Anaheim chiles, roasted (see page 3), peeled, seeded, and diced

8 slices bacon, cooked and chopped

BURGERS

2 pounds 80 percent lean ground beef

2 tablespoons unsalted butter

8 hamburger buns

Kosher salt and black pepper

Pico de Gallo (page 125), for topping

Shredded iceberg lettuce, for topping (optional)

When it comes to smothering your burger in queso, which queso to use is up to you. For instance, my brother favors Canutillo Queso (page 61) while a friend swears by Choriqueso (page 65). I prefer a queso that's revved up with bacon, pickled jalapeños, and roasted chiles. Its smoky, sharp, and earthy notes play well with a slab of juicy, salty beef. Then, add a buttery bun along with pico de gallo and shredded iceberg, and you've got a perfect queso burger.

BACON-GREEN CHILE QUESO BURGER

MAKES 8 SERVINGS

To make the queso, in a medium saucepan, melt the butter over medium-low heat. Add the onion and cook, stirring occasionally, until softened, about 5 minutes.

Whisk together the cornstarch, milk, and water until well combined, then pour into the pan. Bring to a simmer, stirring constantly, and cook for a couple of minutes, until the mixture begins to thicken. Add the cheese, turn down the heat to low, and cook, stirring, until the cheese has melted. Stir in the cumin, salt, cayenne, pickled jalapeños, Anaheims, and bacon. Taste and adjust the seasonings, if you like. Turn off the heat.

To make the burgers, divide the ground beef into eight equal portions and form into balls. In a large cast-iron skillet, melt 1 tablespoon of the butter over medium heat. Working in batches, place the buns,

CONTINUED

cut-side down, in the skillet and cook for 1 to 2 minutes, or until lightly toasted. Transfer the first batch to a plate, add the remaining 1 tablespoon butter to the skillet, and toast the remaining buns. Cover with aluminum foil to keep warm.

Using the same skillet, turn the heat to high. (If you don't have a powerful hood, open a window for ventilation.) Place two balls of meat in the skillet. Cook for 30 seconds, then smash each of them down with a flat spatula to form a patty about 4 inches across. Season the patties with salt and pepper. After 2 minutes, or when the patties have developed a crust on the bottom, flip them and cook for 1 to 2 minutes longer, or until the meat is cooked to your liking. Place each patty on a bun bottom. Repeat with the remaining meat.

Spoon about ¼ cup of queso onto each patty and top with pico de gallo and lettuce, if desired. Cover with the bun tops and serve immediately.

CHICKEN-FRIED STEAK

1 (1½-pound) beef top round steak

1 teaspoon kosher salt

1 teaspoon black pepper

½ teaspoon ground cumin

¼ teaspoon cayenne

1½ cups all-purpose flour

2 large eggs

½ cup whole milk

Vegetable oil, for frying

GRAVY

2 tablespoons diced yellow onion

2 jalapeños, seeded and diced

1 tablespoon cornstarch

1 cup whole milk

8 ounces yellow American cheese, shredded

½ teaspoon ground cumin

½ teaspoon kosher salt

Pico de Gallo (page 125), for topping

Though chicken-fried steak may not be the official state food of Texas (that honor goes to chili), much like barbecue and Tex-Mex, many consider it its own food group. Most chicken-fried steaks come drenched in a cream gravy, but sometimes, when they are feeling a little decadent, folks swap the traditional gravy for a healthy ladle of queso.

▼△▽△▽△▽△▽△▽△▽△▽△▽△▽△▽

CHICKEN-FRIED STEAK WITH QUESO GRAVY

MAKES 4 SERVINGS

To make the chicken-fried steak, cut the round steak into four evenly sized pieces. Pound each piece with a meat tenderizer to a ¼-inch thickness and until almost doubled in surface area.

Stir together the salt, pepper, cumin, and cayenne; sprinkle half of this spice mixture over both sides of the steaks.

Whisk together the flour and remaining spice mixture and pour onto a large plate. Beat the eggs and milk in a bowl wide enough to accommodate the steaks. Coat both sides of one piece of steak with the flour mixture, dip into the egg mixture, dredge in flour again, and place on a second large plate. Repeat with remaining steaks.

Preheat the oven to 200°F and line a baking sheet with aluminum foil.

In a large skillet over medium-high heat, warm 1 inch of vegetable oil to 300°F.

CONTINUED

Working in batches, gently place the steaks in the skillet in a single layer. There will be a lot of popping and hissing, so be careful. After 2 to 3 minutes, or when juices start bubbling out of the top of the steak, use tongs to gently flip the steaks and continue to cook until lightly browned, 3 to 4 minutes longer. Transfer the steaks to the prepared baking sheet and place in the oven to keep warm.

To make the gravy, reserve 1 tablespoon of oil from the skillet, then drain the rest and wipe out the skillet with a paper towel. Return the reserved oil to the skillet and warm over medium-low heat. Add the onion and jalapeños and cook until softened, about 5 minutes.

Whisk together the cornstarch and milk until well combined, then pour into the pan. Bring to a simmer and cook, stirring constantly, for a couple of minutes, until the gravy begins to thicken. Add the cheese and stir in the cumin and salt. Taste and adjust the seasonings, if you like.

Transfer the steaks to individual plates, pour on the queso gravy, dividing it evenly, and top with pico de gallo. Serve immediately.

ICE CREAM

3 cups whole milk

8 ounces cream cheese, softened

1 cup sugar

1 tablespoon fresh lime juice

1 tablespoon vanilla extract

¼ teaspoon kosher salt

CHILE JAM

4 Anaheim chiles, roasted (see page 3), peeled, and seeded

½ cup water

½ cup fresh orange juice, plus 2 tablespoons grated orange zest

¼ cup fresh lime juice

¼ cup apple cider vinegar

¾ cup sugar

¼ teaspoon kosher salt

¼ teaspoon ground cinnamon

1 cup chopped roasted and salted or toasted pecans

Cacique, an ice-cream stand in Las Cruces, New Mexico, serves green chile sundaes, which are composed of creamy vanilla ice cream topped with a piquant green chile marmalade and crunchy, salty pecans. It's not savory, but I believe it technically fits the definition of chile con queso, especially if you make the ice cream with cream cheese, as I do in my adaptation of the treat.

Although both the ice cream and the marmalade are just fine on their own, something extraordinary occurs when they are paired, and it's easy to see why this sweet and spicy concoction is the most popular chile con queso dish in town.

GREEN CHILE & CREAM CHEESE ICE CREAM SUNDAES

MAKES 4 TO 6 SERVINGS

To make the ice cream, combine the milk, cream cheese, sugar, lime juice, vanilla, and salt in a blender and blend until smooth. Refrigerate until cold, about 4 hours. Freeze in an ice-cream maker according to the manufacturer's instructions. Transfer to a container, cover, and freeze until firm, about 2 hours.

To make the chile jam, put a plate in the freezer. Combine the Anaheims, water, orange juice, orange zest, lime juice, vinegar, sugar, salt, and cinnamon in a medium saucepan. Bring to a boil over high heat, turn down the heat to low, and simmer, stirring occasionally, until thickened, about 25 minutes. Turn off the heat, spoon a dollop of the liquid onto the chilled plate, let it sit for a minute, then tilt the plate.

CONTINUED

If the jam is thick and syrupy, it's ready. If not, continue to cook over low heat, stirring occasionally and testing every 5 minutes, until the jam is the right consistency. Pour the jam into a small heatproof container, cover, and refrigerate until set, about 4 hours.

Scoop the ice cream into individual bowls and spoon the chile jam on top, dividing it evenly. Sprinkle with the pecans and serve.

ACCOMPANIMENTS

Here are the salsas and pickles that are used throughout the book and that you will always find in my refrigerator. If you are inclined to fry your own chips and tostadas, I can help you with that, too.

GUACAMOLE

MAKES 2 CUPS

2 ripe avocados, halved, pitted, and peeled

2 serrano chiles, seeded and finely chopped

2 cloves garlic, finely minced

¼ cup chopped fresh cilantro

2 tablespoons fresh lime juice

½ teaspoon kosher salt

Creamy and smooth guacamole is a perfect accompaniment to hot chiles and cheese.

In a bowl and using a fork, mash together the avocados, serranos, garlic, cilantro, lime juice, and salt. Taste and adjust the seasonings, if you like. Serve immediately.

PICO DE GALLO

MAKES 2 CUPS

2¼ cups diced grape tomatoes

2 jalapeños, seeded and diced

¼ cup diced red onion

2 cloves garlic, minced

¼ cup chopped fresh cilantro

1 teaspoon kosher salt

¼ teaspoon ground cumin

2 tablespoons fresh lime juice

1½ teaspoons olive oil

This refreshing salsa makes a hearty, lively addition to chile con queso. It's best the day it's made, but will last a day or two if kept refrigerated. Leftovers go well with chips and on salads.

Mix together the tomatoes, jalapeños, onion, garlic, cilantro, salt, cumin, lime juice, and olive oil until well combined. Taste and adjust the seasonings, if you like. Cover and refrigerate for 30 minutes before serving.

PICKLED JALAPEÑOS

MAKES 1 PINT

6 jalapeños, sliced into ¼-inch rounds

2 cloves garlic, minced

1 tablespoon kosher salt

1 teaspoon mustard seeds

¼ teaspoon ground cumin

½ cup white vinegar

½ cup water

These chiles add a bright, piquant note to most quesos.

Place the jalapeños, garlic, salt, mustard seeds, cumin, vinegar, and water in a medium saucepan. Bring to a boil over high heat, then turn off the heat. Pour the mixture into a clean pint jar. Cover and let steep for 30 minutes. The jalapeños are ready to use immediately, or refrigerate for a few hours for even better flavor. Store in the refrigerator for up to 2 weeks.

GREEN CHILE SALSA VERDE

MAKES ABOUT 1 CUP

¼ pound tomatillos, husked

2 serrano chiles, halved lengthwise and seeded

2 cloves garlic

2 Anaheim chiles, roasted (see page 3), peeled, and seeded

½ cup fresh cilantro

½ teaspoon kosher salt

½ teaspoon ground cumin

Pinch of cayenne (optional)

This tangy salsa makes an appearance in a few recipes in this book and is also a fine dipping sauce on its own.

Place the tomatillos, serranos, and garlic in a saucepan. Cover with water, bring to a boil over high heat, and then turn down the heat to low and simmer for 10 minutes. Turn off the heat and let cool for 10 minutes.

Using a slotted spoon, transfer the tomatillos, serranos, and garlic to a blender. Pour in ½ cup of the cooking water; add the Anaheims, cilantro, salt, and cumin; and puree until smooth. Taste and adjust the seasonings, adding cayenne if you desire it hotter. Store in an airtight container in the refrigerator for up to 1 week.

Vegetable oil, for frying

24 corn tortillas, cut into quarters

Kosher salt

TORTILLA CHIPS

Sure, tortilla chips are readily available, but nothing beats the crisp excellence of a batch fresh out of the fryer. If you have the time and inclination, I suggest making your own at home.

Line a baking sheet with paper towels.

In a large, heavy skillet, warm about ¾ inch vegetable oil over medium-high heat until it reaches 325°F. In small batches (don't crowd the pan), place the tortillas in the hot oil and fry until light brown and crisp, about 30 seconds per side, turning them with a slotted spatula. Transfer the chips to the prepared baking sheet and lightly sprinkle with salt. Serve immediately or store in an airtight container at room temperature for up to 3 days.

CRISPY TOSTADAS
Simply leave the tortillas whole and cook as directed.

MAKES 12 TOSTADAS

Vegetable oil, for frying

12 corn tortillas

Kosher salt

PUFFY TOSTADAS

For years I wanted to make puffy tostadas like the ones you see at Tex-Mex restaurants such as Los Tios in Houston. The light, airy shells with a swollen yet delicate structure somehow manage to support a magnitude of queso. Whenever I attempted to make them at home in New York, however, I could never get them to work. I thought the secret was using raw, just-pressed tortillas. But one day I threw a cooked tortilla into hot oil and was delighted to see it blow up like a balloon. I soon discovered that fresh tortillas made with minimal ingredients are key. The package ingredients should read: corn, lime, and water. If you see fillers, the tortillas are probably too processed to puff. (In the Southwest, you shouldn't have a problem finding good, fresh ones; elsewhere, try Trader Joe's or Whole Foods.)

Although this method is a bit of an art, if you ensure your oil is at 375°F and your corn tortillas are fresh and made without fillers, you'll be well on your way to puffy tostada success. If your first tortilla doesn't inflate, keep trying. It took me years to get it right! To serve puffy tostadas, pour the queso of your choice over the freshly fried tostadas.

Line a baking sheet with paper towels.

In a large skillet, warm 2 inches of vegetable oil over medium-high heat until it reaches 375°F. Place a tortilla in the hot oil and press on the edges with a slotted spatula. After a few seconds, the tortilla should puff up. Gently flip it over and let it cook for 20 seconds longer. Using the spatula, transfer the tostada to the prepared baking sheet and lightly sprinkle with salt. Repeat with the remaining tortillas. Serve immediately.

ACKNOWLEDGMENTS

It always takes quite a few people to put together a book, and here are those who were very helpful in bringing *Queso!* to life.

First, I want to thank my dear friends Monica Crowley and Shelby Walters who one night in Austin listened to my thoughts on queso and thought they would make for a fun book. Their constant nudging to pursue the project convinced me it was a fine idea.

My energetic agent and fellow Texan Brettne Bloom was a prime mover in getting this book out of my head and into your hands. Her assistant at The Book Group, Dana Murphy, has also been very helpful.

It is such an honor to be published by Ten Speed Press, which produces some of my favorite books. Thank you to Emily Timberlake for her sunny enthusiasm, Dawn Yanagihara for making the manuscript shine, Margaux Keres for her beautiful design, and Aubrie Pick for her gorgeous photography. Also instrumental for making this such an outstanding book are Kristin Casemore, Windy Dorrestyn, Allison Renzulli, Ashley Lima, Emma Campion, Heather Porter, Bessma Khalaf, Lillian Kang, Claire Mack, Veronica Laramie, Cortney Munna, Molly Jackel, Abigail Bok, Aaron Wehner, and Hannah Rahill.

As I traveled around learning about queso, I spoke with some people who shared with me their favorite spots and recipes. I am thankful for Cynthia Adrian, Rob Bhatka, Audri Escobedo, Maynard Haddad, Jennifer Holguin, Melanie Lopez, D. J. Martinez, Victoria Ventura, Marshall Wright, John McClure, Cynthia Rey, and Martina Rey for being generous with their queso knowledge.

A big debt of gratitude to librarians John Wilson, Amie Oliver, Brian Simmons, and Tiff Sowell at The Texas Collection at Baylor University and to Amber Harmon at Pace Library at the University of Texas at San Antonio, who pulled countless old cookbooks for me to read.

Here's to my recipe testers who did the difficult work of making queso and providing valuable feedback on the dishes: Lisa Brownlee, Julie Fisher, Ginny Heckel, Dominique Jernigan, Julie Jernigan, Nathan Jernigan, Richard Jernigan, Kirk Justus, Timothy Richardson, and Debra Pearson.

Many thanks to those who provided housing, camaraderie, ideas, and feedback, including John Crowley, Wendy Dominguez, Amy C. Evans, Laura Kopchick, Alex Lewis, Shelley McKinley, Hillary Netardus, Catherine Osborne, and Kelly Yandell.

As always, a big thanks to my grandma, mom, dad, stepmom, brother, sister-in-law, and nephews, who supported me in many ways, including making and eating queso.

Last but not least, I want to thank all of my readers. Without your encouragement and support, this couldn't be possible. Thank you.

ABOUT THE AUTHOR

LISA FAIN is the James Beard Award–winning creator of the blog
Homesick Texan and author of *The Homesick Texan Cookbook*
and *The Homesick Texan's Family Table*. A seventh-generation
Texan, she currently resides in New York City.

INDEX